Hazard Unlimited

Slay Me Suddenly

Dangerfoot

Great Ideas in Communications

David and the Donkey

Red for Remembrance: The British Legion 1921–1971

Who Cares for Animals?: 150 years of the RSPCA

Cuthbert Heath: Maker of the Modern Lloyd's of London

As Anthony Forrest (in collaboration with Norman Mackenzie)

Captain Justice

The Pandora Secret

A Balance of Dangers

HAZARD UNLIMITED

From ships to satellites
300 years of Lloyd's of London
an intimate portrait

———————

ANTONY BROWN

Third Edition

LLOYD'S OF LONDON PRESS LTD
1987

Lloyd's of London Press Ltd.
Sheepen Place, Colchester
Essex CO3 3LP
26–30 Artillery Lane, London E1 7LX

USA AND CANADA
Lloyd's of London Press Inc.
Suite 523, 611 Broadway
New York, NY 10012 U.S.A.

GERMANY
Lloyd's of London Press
PO Box 11 23 47, Deichstrasse 41
2000 Hamburg 11, West Germany

SOUTH EAST ASIA
Lloyd's of London Press (Far East) Ltd.
903 Chung Nam Building
1 Lockhart Road, Wanchai
Hong Kong

©

Antony Brown 1973, 1978, 1987
First published in Great Britain, 1973
Second impression, 1974
Second edition, 1978
Third edition, 1987

British Library Cataloguing in Publication Data
Brown, Antony
Hazard unlimited.——3rd ed.
1. Lloyd's of London——History
I. Title
368'.012' 094212   HG8039

ISBN 1–85044–137–5 (cased)
ISBN 1–85044–131–6 (limp)

Cover design: Alan Mauro, Artform

Typeset in 10pt on 12pt Linotron 202 Ehrhardt by
Promenade Graphics, Cheltenham, Glos.
Printed in Great Britain by
The Eastern Press Ltd., London and Reading

Preface

This book is by no means a history of Lloyd's of London. It is intended simply as a modest guide to the tradition and working of the market. My first aim has been to show the ordinary reader how Lloyd's works, and to catch something of its atmosphere and special flavour.

Readers of previous editions will find that many pages have been considerably up-dated. Some of the underwriters and brokers who figured in the first edition are no longer in the market, which has itself seen some memorable changes since my original researches. The result is that much of the material in this book is appearing for the first time. Meanwhile Lloyd's, despite external change, remains itself. It is my hope that this new edition suggests something of the romance and style which are its inimitable features.

June 1987   ANTONY BROWN

Contents

Illustrations

PART ONE
The Tradition

I

The Room

If you walk from Bank Station towards Leadenhall Street, you will find yourself in one of the City's small worlds. As other parts of the City exist for furs or fish, Leadenhall Street exists for ships. It may be anything from Cunard to the Greek Hull Pool, from P & O to Hispania Marine. In the small streets around St Mary Axe there are so many offices of shipbrokers, ship-insurers and ship-owners that you almost expect the streets themselves to have water in them, like Amsterdam or Venice.

There is Africa House and there was once East India House, and towering above them all is Lloyd's. It has no sign over it and it needs none, for it is less of an office than an institution—the home of the most historic insurance market in the world.

But what really is Lloyd's? Everyone has heard of it, yet few could tell you much about it, except perhaps that it insures ships. The reality is both broader and deeper. This very English institution is global in its interests and outlook. It is also very traditional, yet a key part of the tradition has always been to innovate and pioneer.

In the history of business enterprise there is nothing quite like Lloyd's of London. For the last two hundred years of its history, its heart and centre has been a room called simply *the* Room. Let us begin by seeing what happens in it.

Originally the Room was part of a coffee house in seventeenth century London. Today it is probably Europe's most noted piece of high-tech building whose soaring atrium is one of the sights of modern London. Yet in essence it has not changed. If you go into the Room today you will still see what happened at Lloyd's in the seventeenth century.

You will see underwriters sitting talking to brokers, much as their counterparts did in the coffee house. You will see a man in a red robe, known as the Caller, who intones the names of brokers. His counterpart in the coffee house recited the names of overdue ships, but the principle is the same. There are other red-robed men who in an ordinary business house would be called porters, commissionaires and messengers. At Lloyd's, because of its origins, they are still called waiters.

As you begin to take in the geography of the Room you will see that it has one main feature—the rows of underwriters' boxes. These, too, stem from the coffee house—in essence a box consists of two wooden pews with a table between them. Anything from six to a dozen people can sit in a box, and if you look down on the Room from the fourth-floor viewing area you get the impression of hundreds of separate groups, packed in their boxes like commuters in a crowded train.

Why, you might ask, should Lloyd's cling to this archaic custom? The point is that now, as in the 1760s, Lloyd's is not an insurance office but a market—the only place in the world where you can find so many potential insurers under one roof. The underwriter's box is really his pitch in the market—if a broker cannot place his risk at one box, he moves to another.

If, as often happens, the risk is too big for a single insurer, then the broker will find plenty of others in the Room to take a share of it. Thus he can complete the whole insurance, even on the most complex or large-scale risk, within a single market.

But before we go into the procedure in detail, let us look at the people who, over three hundred years, have made Lloyd's unique: the underwriters.

Once in the 1890s a famous Lloyd's man was asked by a lady visitor to explain the market. He made a celebrated answer. 'Individually, madam,' he said, 'we are underwriters. Collectively, we are Lloyd's.' Over nearly a century the definition has not been bettered—the point is that people work *at* Lloyd's, not for it. The underwriters are answerable for certain things to the Council of Lloyd's, but not for their underwriting. The Council is there to see that the market is properly run, and that its reputation for integrity is maintained. Beyond that, the underwriter is his own man.

Perhaps it is because of the very looseness of the organization that Lloyd's has always evoked a special kind of loyalty. There is a sense of belonging which would be hardly imaginable in a conventional business. Nobody ever thinks of leaving Lloyd's; most members will tell you, without embarrassment, that they love the place.

One famous Lloyd's man described to me how, as a young clerk, he used to dream of the day he might become an underwriter. All underwriters have their own special flourish when putting their initials to a risk; and he had spent hours optimistically practising his own initial. I asked him to show me how it looked, and he wrote it lovingly, like an artist, on a page of my pad. 'I don't known how many times I've written it since then,' he said, 'but I've never lost the sense of magic.'

'Personal friendship and the great liberality I have always found induces me to do my business with them,' said a broker of the underwriters in 1810, and the feeling is still there. One former Lloyd's broker told me a story that had happened years ago, over an August bank holiday. On the Friday before the holiday one of his clients posted him an order for insurance on a cargo of fish that was going to South America. The ship sailed over the weekend and by the time the market opened on Tuesday morning she had gone aground on some rocks off the coast of Portugal.

'In those days,' said the broker, 'there was no such thing as automatic cover, and of course the order for the insurance didn't arrive till the Tuesday morning.' He went to the Room, and sought out the underwriter with whom he would normally have placed the risk. 'He looked me in the eye and asked was this a risk I would normally have brought to him first? I said it was, and he picked up his pen and wrote it—the insurance on a cargo that he knew was already floating out to the Atlantic.'

Once in the eighteenth century the existence of Lloyd's was threatened by the spread of a kind of underwriting which was virtually gambling. A group of Lloyd's men removed themselves from the scene, took the best of the tradition with them and set up the coffee house elsewhere. Again, in the early part of this century when safeguards were less strict than today, Lloyd's integrity was threatened by a defaulting underwriter. Rather than let its good name go down, every man in the market paid a share of what was owing—it amounted to nearly a quarter of a million pounds. In both cases, it could be argued, Lloyd's men were acting in what was ultimately their own interest. But there was also something else—the feeling that the special quality of the place must be preserved at all costs.

Till recently, Lloyd's had the reputation of being a kind of gentlemen's club, but that is true no longer. There are still those who come to Lloyd's because their fathers did, but many more who have come up from being clerks in the Room. I met one underwriter who was descended from the poet Coleridge, and another who was the son of a gas-fitter from Hackney. If there is an élite in the market, it is not social but professional. The boxes you see most crowded with brokers are those of what are known as leading underwriters; there are leading underwriters at Lloyd's whose progress through the Room has something of the verve and dignity of a Renaissance duke.

To be 'leading' in this sense does not mean merely to be prominent. Literally, the leading underwriter 'leads' a risk. This means that he is the first person to whom the broker shows it. With the broker, he will work out the rate for the risk, or even decide it is unacceptable as offered. Though he does not bind the market, he sets a rate for the business. Following underwriters will write their line, or proportion of the risk, at the same rate because they trust his judgement.

The leading underwriter may guide the market but every underwriter is perpetually making decisions. Every moment he is on his box he is assessing a risk. Each time he accepts one, he is backing his decision with his own money. 'They've got to be tougher than nails,' said one visiting American broker. 'There's nobody like a Lloyd's underwriter. It's the lonesomest occupation I know—there's nowhere else where you sit all day at the buckstop.' Perhaps for this reason, modesty is the least apparent virtue in the Room. The underwriters make up the most aggressively intelligent insurance market in the world, and know it.

Because of its intense individualism there is none of the rigid orthodoxy that you find in most City institutions—at Lloyd's, you feel, they like to be a little unpredictable. One very obvious example was their choice of Europe's most noted *avant-garde* architect to design their present building. Another, smaller but equally significant, was that not long ago the members elected as chairman an underwriter whose political views were known to be radical: it was the kind of mildly unconventional touch that Lloyd's men rather like. Several members of Lloyd's own race-horses. A lot, particularly marine underwriters, have boats. 'You wouldn't think messing about in a fourteen-foot dinghy could help you to insure an oil tanker,' said one, 'but it's surprising what you can learn about wind and weather.'

In a way such details are a pointer to Lloyd's style—if the underwriters have a professional credo, it would be a mixture of accumulated expertise, flair and the acquisition of odd bits of useful knowledge.

Often they have a touch of temperament unusual in the City; along with the style and charm there is an edge of gritty toughness, and because of the immaculacy of the charm it is not always easy to discern which characteristic is overlaying which. At one box I listened while a broker tried to convince the underwriter that a particular client of his was a reformed character. This ship-owner, he said, had come to London and had lunch at the broker's office, and explained how he had spent the whole winter re-equipping his fleet.

Despite the broker's pleading, the underwriter had got his head down. 'He may have had lunch with you,' he said. 'He's still a crook.'

The broker laughed, as if the underwriter must be allowed his joke, but after another twenty minutes they were still talking. Later I asked the underwriter what would happen about the risk and he said he did a lot of business with that particular broking firm, and you had to keep a good relationship going. 'It's not the sort of thing you can have spoilt by a difficult client,' he said. 'In the end I'll probably write it.'

It would mean something to a Lloyd's man if you told him that a non-marine name had written a wet risk: like all highly individual atmospheres, the Room has its own jargon. You can get to know a good deal about the market without ever learning the difference between a deductible and excess-of-loss. What you do need to know is that the underwriter never signs a policy, he writes it—as other people might write books or sonnets, Lloyd's underwriters write jet airliners and nuclear power-stations. The piece of paper the broker shows him is called a Slip. If he accepts the risk on the slip he writes what is called his Line, or proportion of the insurance. When he does this he is accepting the risk for his Syndicate which is composed of what are known as Names—or what other businesses would call his sleeping partners.

Apart from direct risks, the slip the broker offers may be for Reinsurance. It may sound paradoxical, but an underwriter, having taken on a risk, will often seek to unload some of his liability. To do this he reinsures with another syndicate—thus making certain that if there is a loss it will not be more than his syndicate can bear. Often the client in such a case will be an outside insurance company—Lloyd's, as the largest market of this kind in the world, reinsures not only British companies but most of the leading American ones.

All this, like much else in the Room, we shall come back to. Meanwhile there is something else which is at the heart of the tradition—an almost restlessly inventive urge to pioneer. It was a Lloyd's underwriter who wrote the first burglary risk in the early part of this century. Today the risk is more likely to be on pollution in California or a new kind of drilling-rig in the Arctic, but Lloyd's response is the same—to try to work out a way of insuring something that the rest of the insur-

ance world is sill alarmed by. 'Of course it's a profitable business,' said
one underwriter, 'and I wouldn't be in it if I wasn't making money. But
I wouldn't be in it either if it wasn't fun.'

Another underwriter said that the whole point was that at Lloyd's
there was no such thing as a fixed rate: if you went to an ordinary
insurance company they would look it up in a book, but at Lloyd's
every rate and every risk was different. Some time before, he said, a
broker had come and asked him if he would write a risk on a railroad in
America, and his deputy on the box had said they didn't write railroads. 'I said the hell with it, the rules are there to be broken. So we
started writing railroads, and we've made a healthy profit.'

If there were such a thing as a typical Lloyd's man of the 1980s, he
might be a bit like Terry Pitron, the aviation underwriter for the Secretan syndicate, which was founded by a Swiss who came to London
during the Napoleonic Wars. Terry Pitron himself is a trim, deft-
looking man with rather strongly chiselled features and the decisive
manner which people tend to acquire as underwriters. He has been at
Lloyd's since 1952, and loves it. As he approaches Box 122 you sense
his perceptions sharpening, like an actor about to go on stage. Sometimes, he says, he can wake up in the morning feeling dejected about
the business. 'Then when I go into the Room it's all right. We have to
be performers.'

The box itself is like a small world. Perhaps because most of the
other seven people are young, I sensed a sort of family atmosphere
over which Pitron presides like a kindly but commanding parent. I slid
into the seat next to him, facing a row of record books and several bags
of sweets which Pitron offered to the brokers as they came up. Facing
him sat his deputy, Robert Swinton, who came straight to Lloyd's from
Purley Grammar School. Two of the six people on the box, I learnt
had been to public schools, and only one was a graduate. Few people
working in the Room nowadays have got there through family connections.

At half past two there was already a stream of brokers drifting back
from lunch. At Box 122 there was a small queue of them, their slip-
cases bulging with their afternoon's wares. The first broker in line sat
down on the small flap-seat on the other side of Terry. His risk was for
a charter company, based in Sweden, which planned to fly British
tourists to the Canary Islands. The aircraft they were using were
Viscounts, at which Terry cocked an eyebrow.

'Why are they using Viscounts, not jets or modern turbo-props?'

The broker began to glow with confidence about the Viscounts. They might be old, he said, but Terry should remember them as very safe, efficient aircraft. The pilots were British, and the company had gone to great lengths to train them on the Viscounts.

Terry asked a cautious question about the availability of spares, then picked up his pen, which is the moment they say the broker should stop talking, and wrote 'Secretan 1%' with a broad, sweeping, self-confident brush-stroke from the pen's big flat oblique nib. Most underwriters still use ink-pens and keep pink blotting-paper by them.

Then he picked up the stamp which bears—even though it is an aircraft policy—Lloyd's anchor-sign, 545, the number of the syndicate, and the letters TOP.

'What does TOP mean?'

'That's referred to as the syndicate's pseudonym. It doesn't mean I'm top underwriter,' said Terry, amid some laughter from his young staff. 'It's my initials.'

Across the box Robert was being asked to insure an aircraft that he didn't seem to like the sound of. He looked it up in Jane's *Pocket Aviation Guide*, and then turned to the broker. 'I think I can live prosperously without writing this one.'

'I'm sure you can, sir.' Brokers have a way of sounding particularly courteous when they feel hard done by. Meanwhile Terry himself was now being asked to write a policy for an American corporation which manufactures undercarriage gear used in F111s and helicopters. The company had been in business for twenty-one years, said the broker confidently, with only one loss.

'Very iffy kind of risk,' Terry turned to me, explaining that this was a question of product liability. If there was a crash and the landing gear was found faulty, the manufacturer might be held liable in the courts. 'We generally seek to avoid products on helicopters,' he said.

The broker said that the only way you could look at it was that the premium had gone up from $270,000 to $480,000. In the end Terry wrote it. 'Technically the difference between a good risk and a bad is premium, or lack of it,' he said. 'Also he's a good broker, with a good account. We like to encourage them to come back.'

The next risk was for third party only, on what Terry called a geriatric jet. 'Third party only, that means liability coverage if it hits other aircraft or property or people on the ground.' He asked Annemarie, one of the two girls on the box, to hand him the claims record on the risk in question. 'I don't think there's much in it for me. Besides, they make big holes when they crash,' he said delicately, offering the broker a boiled sweet by way of consolation.

The broker made encouraging noises about the premium, then seemed to sense that Terry was determined. 'Thank you very much,' Terry said politely. The broker observed rather drily that he wished he could say the same, and moved off. Before the next customer came in, Terry told me that apart from the big holes, the amount of premium meant there was nothing in it for him—a lot of risk for very little premium.

By now there were three more brokers in the queue. The first spread his slip across the desk: a war risk for a major US airline, it had so many noughts on the liability cover that they ran into the next line. 'This year the fleet value is around three billion dollars,' said the broker.

Terry looked interested, but observed that this airline had had two losses last year because of hijacks. 'Have they tightened their security, bearing in mind our Middle East friends?'

The broker said something about changing routes to avoid flying over Afghanistan and Iran, but by now Terry had his pen poised. Next, by way of contrast, came a small UK charter fleet; again Annemarie passed him the claims record, which he showed me. 'This was last year. They had a claim from a lady passenger who got scalded with hot coffee. That'd be funny if it wasn't serious. When did you last get hot coffee in an aircraft?' Among the other claims was one for engine damage by what was described as bird ingestion, while another engine had been struck by an airport tractor when it was being serviced. Bearing in mind the five-year record, he said, he might write five per cent as against two per cent last year, which pleased the broker. Next year, he said, it would probably be more again, because the Secretan syndicate was expanding rapidly and there would be a lot of new names to write for.

There was a pause in the stream of brokers, and he began telling me how the decisive manner could brush off on an underwriter's general way of life, for example when he got home. 'That's one of the things you have to watch,' he said. 'You get home after a day when you've been anticipating what the broker's going to say, and there's some home or school problem. You tend to snap out yes or no, and the family think you're being impatient.' I asked what his other interests were outside his family and work. It seemed he played squash a bit, and this evening a client was taking him to a cup-tie at White Hart Lane, but in general, he said, work was his main interest. There was no time for more sidelights on an underwriter's domestic life, for another broker loomed up. This time it was an older, jolly-looking man whom Terry asked if he'd had a nice holiday and complimented on his suntan.

The broker said that since Terry seemed in an amiable mood, he might like to write two aircraft which belonged to a Third World country's national defence force. They only flew on special occasions, carrying VIPs.

'Excludes combat, does it?'

The broker said of course it bloody did, and would Terry do as much as he could, perhaps two and a half per cent?

'One and a half,' said Terry firmly, giving him a boiled sweet.

By now the market was thinning out, the brokers returning to their offices, where they would catch up with their phone calls, and the underwriters going to tea, followed by another hour's work. Terry looked at his watch and said he'd be going early this evening, for the Tottenham match. I thanked him and said goodbye, then strolled back past the casualty boards where the clerks were noting down the details of fires, shipwrecks, all the imaginable and unimaginable disasters against which Lloyd's insures the world. Soon the great Room would be empty as a silent theatre. There would be nothing but crumpled pink blotting paper in the aisles and the ghosts, if the underwriters have ghosts, straying from the shadows.

It seemed a moment to pause, and look back to the beginning.

The New Lloyd's—
the Atrium seen from
Leadenhall Market

Underwriting boxes
in the Room

Part of the Nelson
Plate: the vase
awarded to Lord
Northcote, third-in-
command at
Trafalgar

The Rostrum—note
the clock at 12.45—it
is a favourite meeting
place at lunchtime

2

The Coffee House

To think of a coffee house as a place of business requires a certain effort of the imagination. One can imagine a folk-opera being written within range of a modern Gaggia machine, but hardly the insurance of a ship's hull. Yet in seventeenth-century London the coffee house was something between a specific market place and a club. The regular customer would have a comfortable chair by the fire. He would be waited on, most likely, by a pretty waitress. Not only was the actual coffee or kauphy, as it was known, non-intoxicating; it was, according to the advertisements, positively life-giving. 'It is excellent', ran the advertisement for Pasqua Rosee's coffee house in St Michael's Alley, off Cornhill, 'to prevent and cure the dropsy, gout and scurvy. It is known by experience to be better than any other drying drink for people in years, or children that have any running humours upon them, as the king's evil, etc. It is a most excellent remedy against the spleen, hypochondriac winds, and the like. It will prevent drowsiness, and make one fit for business.'

The contemporary copywriter's use of words in the last phrase was particularly well aimed—above all, the coffee house was the place where a man would conduct his business. Of London's 300 coffee houses in the reign of Charles II, most catered for a specific group. For the poets and wits of Covent Garden, there was Button's, the Bedford, and Will's, where Dryden had his own chair. The doctors would go to Child's in St Paul's Churchyard, close to the Royal College of Surgeons. For the lawyers there were the coffee houses on the south side of Fleet Street; the scholars and journalists went to the Grecian on the north side. Nearer Temple Bar was the evidently notorious Rainbow, whose proprietor was charged, in 1657, with 'making and selling a sort of liquor called Kauffee, being a great nuisance and prejudice to the neighbourhood'.

For the merchants and bill brokers in the city there was Hain's in Birchin Lane, or Garraway's where they sold ships by the old method of candle-auctions. Bidding would go on while the candle burnt down an inch. A pin would be stuck in the bottom of it and the last bid had to be made before the pin dropped out as the surrounding candle melted. It must have been a dramatic sight, the faces of the bidders lit by candlelight in the silence during which—as the phrase has come down to us—you could hear a pin drop.

Sometimes—and in these days before Lloyd's it seems likely to have happened most often at Garraway's—a merchant in some other line of business would set up a small sideline of insuring ships. In the nature of things there were probably few of these insurers, or underwriters as they were historically known from the fact that they wrote their line and proportion of the risk under each other's. So we can imagine the underwriter sitting by the fire at Garraway's, or the broker with a risk to place hawking it from one coffee house to another, probably from Garraway's to Jonathan's, from Jonathan's to the Barbadoes coffee house in Change Alley.

But on the whole that is about all we can safely imagine. From those early days of underwriting, hardly a record has come down. Just occasionally we have the details of an actual deal. Truthful to his diary if nothing else, Samuel Pepys records how he once passed up the opportunity of making a dishonest penny:

Up and to Alderman Backewell's where Sir W. Rider, by appointment, met us to consult about the insuring of our hempe ship from Archangell . . . Back to the Coffee-house, and then to the 'Change where Sir W. Rider and I did bid 15 per cent., and nobody will take it under 20 per cent., and the lowest was 15 per cent., premium, and 15 more to be abated in case of losse, which we did not think fit without order to give . . . called at the Coffee-house, and there by great accident hear that a letter is coming that our ship is safe come to Newcastle. With this news I went like an asse, presently to Alderman Backewell and told him of it . . . Now what an opportunity had I to have concealed this and seemed to have made an insurance and got £100 with the least trouble and danger in the whole world. This troubles me to think I should be so oversoon.

The date of that diary entry is 23 November 1663. Three years later came the Great Fire, and an end to the physical geography of the city as Pepys and his contemporaries had known it.

Gradually, through the next two decades, the ruined areas began to be rebuilt. But the new houses round the Royal Exchange were of stone, and consequently commanded high rents. The result was that a new centre of commerce sprang up at the eastern end of the city—the part which lies roughly between Leadenhall Street and the Tower, and which had been largely untouched by the Fire of London. It was in this area, in Tower Street off Eastcheap, that Edward Lloyd began his coffee house somewhere in the 1680s.

Who was Edward Lloyd? And why did his coffee house come to be linked with marine insurance?

The answer to the second question is relatively easy—the coffee house was close to the Tower and what is now the Pool of London. Its location alone must have made it a natural meeting place for seamen, ships' captains and ship-owners.

Of Edward Lloyd himself we know almost nothing. He seems to have been born around 1648, to have been a church warden, and three times married. He was a member of the Framework Knitters' Company, membership of which may have come down to him through his father. When he died in 1713 he was buried in St Mary Woolnoth's in Lombard Street.

What we do know about Lloyd, though, is that his business seems to have prospered from the beginning. By 1688, at least, it must have been well known. For in that year we find the first written reference to Lloyd's, in an advertisement in the *London Gazette*.

The advertisement was inserted by one Edward Bransby of Derby, who had apparently been robbed of five watches and was offering a guinea reward to anyone who could give information about the theft.

Edward Bransby of Derby must have been an observant man, for he described the thief in detail—middle-sized, with black, curled hair and pockholes, not to mention a beaver hat and a brown riding-coat. Whether Bransby ever got his watches back we do not know. The point is that in his advertisement he asked for any information about the thief to be reported to Lloyd's. By 1688 the coffee house must have been at least well enough known to occur to a citizen of Derby as a place which anyone in London would be likely to find.

Three years later in 1691, we find Lloyd moving to much larger and presumably more expensive premises in Lombard Street. Here the coffee house was to remain for the next eighty years—years when the foundation of Lloyd's as a centre of marine insurance would be laid.

It is worth noting that at no stage was Lloyd himself concerned with the actual business of insuring ships. His role was simply to provide a coffee house. True, he must have become fairly knowledgeable about marine insurance, but only in the sense that one might expect the secretary of the Athenaeum to be well informed about bishops.

All the same, Edward Lloyd was clearly a man of reputation. In 1703, for instance, when Britain was at war and nobody could leave the country without a passport, his name comes up as a reference fifteen times in three months. Germans bound for the Hanseatic ports, Englishmen going to the West Indies, seem all to have asked Lloyd to vouch for their credentials.

There were less respectable trades as well. A newspaper of 2 January 1793 carried this advertisement:

A negro maid aged about sixteen years, named Bess, having on a stript stuff waistcoat and peticoat, is much peck't with the Small Pox, and hathe lost a piece of her left ear, speaks English well, ran away from her Master Captain Benjamin Quelch, on Tuesday, the 8th of December. A Guinea for anybody delivering her to Mr Edward Lloyd.

Such dabblings in the slave trade were probably taken for granted by the kind of people who frequented Edward Lloyd's. Meanwhile there were other and more admirable ways in which he seems to have gone beyond his role as the proprietor of a coffee house, and it was these, more than anything, which were the key to his success.

All coffee houses saw it as their duty to supply their customers with pens and ink, but Edward Lloyd went one further. He supplied them with news. He employed runners who would work from the coffee house down to the wharves, picking up the news of ship arrivals. When there were casualties which might be important to his customers, an announcement would be made to the coffee house at large by one of the waiters who was known as the Kidney. 'It is the custom at Lloyd's,' wrote Steel in the *Tatler*, 'upon the first coming in of the news, to order a youth, who officiates as the *Kidney* of the coffee house, to get into the pulpit, and read every paper with a loud and distinct voice, while the whole audience are sipping their respective liquors.'

By 1696, Lloyd's whole conception of a news and intelligence service had gone much further. By then if a ship-owner in the West Country wanted to sell a ship, he would send an inventory and description of her to Lloyd's, and put an advertisement in the daily papers telling prospective customers that further particulars might be had at the coffee house in Lombard Street.

From here the next step was clear. In 1696 Lloyd brought out his own newspaper of shipping movements. Under the title *Lloyd's News* it was, the imprint said, 'Printed for Edward Lloyd (Coffee man) in Lombard Street'.

Modest as the imprint sounds, Lloyd must by now have been in a booming way of business, with his coffee house the acknowledged centre for anyone concerned with ships. Somewhere, probably early on in the Lombard Street days, the chairs and tables had come to be replaced by boxes for the customers to sit at.

Soon the pulpit from which the Kidney addressed the customers was being used for auctions too. The candle sales, once famous at Garraway's, now took place at Lloyd's, and as early as 1692 there is a reference to a sale by candle at Lloyd's of three ships from as far away as 'Plimmouth'. There were sales of Turkey coffee, Alicant wines, and even horses.

By 1700 the sales had become an everyday feature of London life— so much so that the author of a contemporary doggerel called *The Wealthy Shopkeeper and Charitable Citizen* wrote of his hero that he went:

> Now to Lloyd's Coffee House: he never fails
> To read the letters and attend the Sales.

By the turn of the century, in fact, we can begin to see the first shadowy outline of the modern Lloyd's. The coffee house had become a centre for everything which could be called maritime—shipping news, ship sales, ships' cargoes. Already the setting and the props were there, the pulpit and benches which were forerunners of the boxes. So were the small-part players like the Kidney, later to become the Caller.

What was still missing was the central figure—the Lloyd's underwriter.

Long before 1700 people had been insuring ships. Probably the Greeks and Phoenicians had insured against maritime loss, but the first existing record comes from a Roman edict of AD 533, in the reign of the Emperor Justinian. It fixed the interest on all loans at six per cent but made an exception for the rate of marine insurance. This was allowed to go as high as twelve per cent—the practice of usury being thus restrained, wrote Gibbon, 'except in this perilous adventure'.

Over the centuries various forms of marine insurance flicker and fade across the skyline of our knowledge. We learn that the Hanseatic merchants of northern Europe had an insurance centre based at Bruges. In 1432 the city of Barcelona laid down the first recorded statute for insuring ships. In those days when a vessel was lost, the circumstances of her loss were seldom known. If a ship had not been heard of for six months, said the statute of Barcelona, she would be regarded as lost, and the owner could claim from the insurer.

Meanwhile the first form of marine insurance in Britain had been started by a group of Hanseatic merchants who came to London in the fourteenth century. In those days Britain had hardly begun to be a trading nation. The Germans seem to have come as somewhat unwelcome colonists, and to have been treated as such by the Londoners. To protect them from attacks by the mob, they were allowed a piece of land on the site of what is now Cannon Street Station.

Here they proceeded to build a kind of fortification rather grimly known as the Steelyard. Within it they carried on every conceivable kind of business and lived a depressingly disciplined life. They ate communally, were not allowed to marry or even visit women, and the Steelyard door was firmly barred at night.

Few spectacles are less attractive than that of someone trying to make a lot of money when he has nothing agreeable to spend it on, and there is something a little unnerving about the thought of these celibate Germans immured behind their fortress in the Steelyard. All the same they have their place in history as London's first underwriters. Working along the lines laid down by the Hanseatic League, they carried on their business throughout the reign of Queen Elizabeth, but in their later years had the competition of another group of foreign immigrants. These were the Lombards, who had been expelled from Italy in the thirteenth century and had built up a flourishing business centre in London by the sixteenth. From them we get the name of Lombard Street and the word *polizza*—a promise—from which our word 'policy' derives. Writing of the site of the Royal Exchange, the London historian John Stow records that 'here anciently the Lombards or Bankers dwelt, and so they did to the days of Queen Elizabeth'.

The last words are significant. By Elizabeth's reign the merchants of London no longer needed to be taught their trade by the Lombards or the Germans. A recent Chairman of Lloyd's observed that in the twentieth century an emergent country needed two symbols of its independence—a national airline and a national insurance company. In Elizabethan England there was something of the same spirit, and at the opening of the Queen's first Parliament in 1559 Sir Nicholas Bacon had asked: 'Is there any, think you, so mad that, having a range of houses in peril of fire, would not gladly pluck down part to have the rest preserved and saved? Doth not the wise merchant in every adventure of danger, give part to have the rest assured?'

Twelve years before Bacon's speech, the first surviving English marine policy had been issued. It was taken out by a man named John Broke, on a ship called the *Santa Maria*, bound with a cargo of wine from Cadiz to London. On Broke's policy there were only two under-writers, but as time went on the numbers grew. By 1555 we find as many as twenty-five underwriters putting their names to a risk.

Who were these underwriters of the Elizabethan age? Most were probably bankers and moneylenders writing insurance as a sideline. But a little later there occurs the name of the first professional insur-ance man in Britain: Richard Candeler, who in 1574 was granted a patent or monopoly of 'all manner of assewrances polleycies intima-cions Renunciacions and other thinges whatsoever . . . upon any shippe or shippes goods or merchaundize'.

By the middle of the seventeenth century the number of under-writers was growing. In the Bodleian Library at Oxford there is a broker's account book containing thirty-one notes of risks and pre-miums written by underwriters scattered around the City from Mark Lane to Threadneedle Street and Crutched Friars. Over the next thirty years one can imagine them shifting their base of operations to Edward Lloyd's coffee house, first by the Tower and then in Lombard Street.

Yet in the years immediately following Lloyd's move to Lombard Street, our knowledge of the underwriters is still vague. Here and there we get a flash of insight. We learn that one Daniel Foe nearly ruined himself by writing marine insurance. (Later he was to put his nautical interest to better use by writing, in the other sense, *Robinson Crusoe*.)

Somewhere in the early 1700s we come across a dark story of a broker's fraud on a ship called the *Vansittart*. Unable, or perhaps not wanting, to complete his risk, the broker had invented two fictitious names of insurers and put them on the slip. The *Vansittart* went down, and the broker was found out.

The repercussions of this affair seem to have gone on long after-wards. As late as 1717 we find a group of office-keepers (as brokers were usually called at the time) defending themselves against the charge that such practices still happened:

We do in answer to such foul false and malicious a charge declare that we detest all such vile actions and do challenge all the merchants in England to produce one instance of any policy made in either of our offices underwrote with a fictitious name . . . The policy hinted at on the *Vansittart* was made by a person since dead who was not an office-keeper but one who acted as a broker for discounting notes and did sometimes make policies.

Meanwhile, when names were written on an insurance slip, whose names were they? Was the marine underwriter's trade still a sort of sideline to some other business? Or had a new kind of figure appeared—an individual underwriter whose profession it was to write insurance, and especially insurance on ships?

All the evidence suggests that he had. And during the next few years his struggle for survival was to be crucial in the making of Lloyd's.

Over the years that led up to 1720 a new element had been thrown into the situation. This was the demand for the setting up of new insurance companies under Royal Charter—an answer, so it was thought, to the frenzy and speculation that had gripped the City of London since the South Sea Bubble. Among the speculators there had been a vast proliferation of small companies seeking to cash in on insurance against everything from fires—presumably fashionable since 1666—to highway robbery. You could get policies against death from gin-drinking, against being lied to by your business competitors, even a policy on what was delicately described as Female Chastity.

In effect the call for new chartered companies meant the end of these speculative insurers. Most probably they deserved to go down—but the trouble was that under the new plan, the individual underwriters seemed bound to go down with them. Given the prospect of large new companies operating under a Royal Charter, there seemed no chance of any individual underwriters surviving.

To the astonished delight of the underwriters, this was not how things turned out. In 1720 charters were granted to two new companies, the Royal Exchange and London Assurance. Both charters laid down that marine insurance could not be written by any other company or corporation.

But—and this is the point—there was no exclusion of individual underwriters. Ironically, they had been immensely helped by the very thing which had seemed bound to destroy them.

Why had this happened? Perhaps the potential power of the individual underwriters had been overlooked in the general concern to put a stop to the mushroom companies. Possibly those who had drafted the Act had been so certain of the new chartered companies' success that they had scarcely bothered about a few individuals who intended to write marine business. Almost by an accident of law, it seemed, the individual underwriter had been given his own charter too. From now on he could write marine business free from the competition of the small companies.

There was only one proviso—in the event of a loss, the whole of the underwriter's accumulated premiums were to be made available to satisfy the assured.

For the future of Lloyd's, the guarantee would be prophetic.

Almost immediately it became clear that the competition from the two new chartered companies was going to be far less of a threat than the individual underwriters had feared. From the start both the London Assurance and the Royal Exchange found themselves in difficulties, largely due to their fishing in the troubled waters of the South Sea Bubble. Moreover neither of them seemed to be so skilled or even interested in marine insurance as they were in fire business. Soon the individual underwriters who met at Lloyd's found themselves writing something like nine-tenths of all the marine insurance business in the City.

Essentially this growing success was based on two things. First there was the law which had excluded the small companies. Second there was the ineffectiveness of the London Assurance and the Royal Exchange.

But there was a third point, almost as important—convenience. Before Lloyd's, and even in the early days of Tower Street, a broker could never be sure where he could find someone who would write a risk, or part of a risk, on a ship.

Now, with the increased standing of Lloyd's as a centre, he could be sure. And long before there was any kind of formal association, the Lombard Street coffee house had become what Lloyd's still is today: a market place where a broker can place his risk without going outside one building.

Beyond the narrow confines of the City other factors were also making for change. Maritime trade was expanding. New trading centres like Birmingham and Manchester needed outlets for their goods to go to the world. Britain had reached a pre-eminence in trade unparalleled since the days of Elizabeth. At Lloyd's in Lombard Street, the heady smell of success must have mingled with the aromatic scent of coffee.

Meanwhile at the coffee house itself there had been changes; the winter of 1712–13 seems to have been a fairly dramatic one in the Lloyd family. In the October, Edward Lloyd's second wife died, and the following month he had married his third wife, Martha. In January his daughter Handy had married her father's head waiter William Newton—possibly Newton had an eye to the main chance and his master's failing health, for two months after the wedding Edward Lloyd died.

Whatever Newton's motives, he did not enjoy the ownership of the coffee house for long. Within a year of Lloyd's death he himself was dead. Handy, following family tradition, got married again, this time to Samuel Shepherd, who remained master of the coffee house till 1727.

Shepherd was succeeded by Thomas Jemson, who deserves a place in any story of Lloyd's if only because it was during his time that *Lloyd's List* made its first appearance. Edward Lloyd himself, you may remember, had begun a newspaper of shipping news in 1696. *Lloyd's News* had survived for a year and then ceased publication. Possibly Jemson had seen a copy of the original *News*—or possibly he was simply catering for the growing need of his customers. In any case he brought out the first edition of the new paper in 1734. No copies earlier than 1740 have come down to us, but in that issue, there is a mention of the fact that from now on, instead of appearing weekly, it will be 'published every Tuesday and Friday. Subscriptions are taken at Three Shillings per Quarter, at the Bar of Lloyd's coffee house in Lombard Street.'

The new publication was clearly a good deal more professional than the somewhat rough-and-ready notes of ships' arrivals which Edward Lloyd had completed with the help of runners from Shadwell and Wapping or the gossip of ships' captains. By now Lloyd's must have already been beginning to build up its network of correspondents who, by the 1780s, would be sending lists of arrivals, sailings and casualties from all the British and Irish ports. Till the end of the eighteenth century the form of *Lloyd's List* would remain unchanged, with the solitary addition on the front page of the time of high water at London Bridge, 'taken from Mr Flamstead's correct Tide Table.'

Meanwhile, what about the actual business of insuring ships? The War of the Austrian Succession brought new hazards to the underwriters. D. E. W. Gibb, Lloyd's historian, writes that by the early 1740s 'the loss of our merchant tonnage was alarming . . . In the later stages of the war the losses became a good deal heavier for two hundred and ninety-seven ships were captured in 1748, three hundred and seven in 1744, and in 1747 no less than four hundred and fifty-seven. And by far the greater part of the financial loss was carried by Lloyd's underwriters.'

Faced with this, there was not much the underwriters could do, except what a Lloyd's man would do in the same situation today—pay up as cheerfully as possible, and put up the premiums. At the same time, another more insidious threat was looming. This was the new attack of the gambling frenzy which had gripped the City in the 1710s.

At first sight it might seem unlikely that gambling should have had much to do with people whose job was marine insurance. But what we have to remember is that for much of the eighteenth century gambling was a kind of national addiction. Later in the century, Walpole wrote that young men of fashion would often lose £10,000 in an evening at the whist and faro banks of Brook's and Almack's.

Edward Gibbon once worked out Charles James Fox's gambling losses and calculated that over a period the Whig leader would lose around £500 an hour. Nor was the fever limited to addicts like Fox or a group of hell-raisers. Even so gentle and moral a character as William Wilberforce once decided he must curb his love of the tables, but even then he only made a resolution to limit his losses to £50 a session.

By the 1760s the contagion had spread to Lloyd's. In 1763 the coffee house had passed into the possession of one Thomas Lawrence, who seems to have been the weakest and least effective in the long succession of masters.

Whether Lawrence encouraged the gambling, or simply did not try to stop it, we do not know. But certainly by 1768 it was threatening Lloyd's whole reputation. It was possible to get a policy—which was a dignified way of saying a bet—on almost anything. You could get a policy on whether there would be a war with France or Spain, whether John Wilkes would be arrested or die in jail, or whether some Parliamentary candidate would be elected. Underwriters offered premiums of 25 per cent on George II's safe return from Dettingen; there were policies on whether this or that mistress of Louis XV would continue in favour or not.

One particularly grisly form of speculation, quoted by Thomas Mortimer in a book published in 1781 and engagingly entitled *The Mystery and Iniquity of Stock Jobbing*, was this:

A practice likewise prevailed of insuring the lives of well-known personages as soon as a paragraph appeared in the newspapers, announcing them to be dangerously ill. The insurance rose in proportion as intelligence could be procured from the servants, or from any of the faculty attending, that the patient was in great danger. This inhuman sport affected the minds of men depressed by long sickness; for when such persons, casting an eye over a newspaper for amusement, saw that their lives had been insured in the Alley at 90 per cent, they despaired of all hopes; and thus their dissolution was hastened.

It is possible that at Lloyd's such activities were limited to a few. Even so, the whole reputation of the coffee house was endangered.

Fortunately for Lloyd's, a group of the more conscientious and far-sighted underwriters saw the danger. In 1769 they began negotiations with Thomas Fielding, one of Lawrence's waiters. The idea was that Fielding should set up a new establishment under the name of New Lloyd's Coffee House. Before the end of the year this breakaway group had found premises at Number 5, Pope's Head Alley.

For the next two years a sort of private warfare seems to have gone on between the old Lloyd's and the new. It was true that Lawrence still had the name and the facilities, which included the publication of *Lloyd's List* and the other shipping intelligence. It was also true that his premises were far better equipped than the Pope's Head Alley house, which was small, inconvenient and draughty. Indeed from the beginning the underwriters seem to have regarded it as little better than a staging post till they could find something better.

But Fielding's coffee house, for all its discomfort, drew the nucleus of the underwriters who had made Lloyd's. And this, in the event, was to be decisive.

For a while attacks and counter-attacks went on in the public announcements column of the press. Then gradually it became clear that the New Lloyd's group were gaining the ascendant. Before long they were publishing their own version of *Lloyd's List*. Inevitably, the business at Lombard Street began to dwindle.

Meanwhile the events of 1769 had been considerably more than a change of scene. What they implied above all was a movement by the underwriters themselves to determine their own future. Fielding as master of the coffee house had an important role, but it was no longer the key role it had been in the past. At the end of 1771 a group of seventy-nine underwriters and brokers set down what has been called the most important document in Lloyd's history: 'We the Underwritten do agree to pay our Several Subscriptions into the Bank of England in the Names of a Committee to be chosen by Ballot for the Building A New Lloyd's Coffee House.'

What was important was not simply the quest for a new building—it was that at last Lloyd's was operating as a group with a common interest. Nine years later when the committee published its first-ever List of Members, it was significantly entitled 'A List of Subscribers to Lloyd's *from the Foundation in 1771*'.

If 1771 is therefore the date for the beginning of the modern Lloyd's, the events of the next two years were hardly less important. From 1772 we have the first minute-books of the newly formed committee. In the following year we come to something else which is a Lloyd's landmark. This time it is not from Lloyd's own records, but from the minutes of a sub-committee of the Mercers' Company, the owners of the Royal Exchange: 'Mr Angurstine [*sic*] from the gentlemen who attend New Lloyd's Coffee house Attended to be informed if there was any large room to be lett over the Exchange. The Committee Ordered the Clerk with the Surveyor to let Mr Angurstine view the two Rooms late in lease to the British Fishery.'

The Clerk to the Sub-Committee of the Mercers' Company can be forgiven for not getting the right spelling of what must have seemed to him an unusual name. John Julius Angerstein was not, in 1773, even a member of the committee of Lloyd's.

On that day, however, something historic had happened. The underwriters and the brokers at Lloyd's had not merely found the new accommodation they were seeking. They had also found the man who, from then till the end of the century, was largely to shape their fortunes.

'Individually we are underwriters but collectively we are Lloyd's.' In one sense Lloyd's can be described as a loosely organized association of people with business interests in common, working together under a common roof.

But there the implication of equality ends. In the eighteenth century as now, Lloyd's depended on a few individuals far-sighted enough to see not merely the next step but the one beyond it.

In the Room today there are perhaps twenty underwriters who will lead a risk, knowing that the rest of the market will follow. This is not just a question of deciding to take a chance. Very often the kind of insurance they are writing will be something new, tailored to a special need, and the terms of it will have been hacked out in endless discussions between them and the broker. It is the sense of innovation which is at the heart of Lloyd's, and through the centuries it has been carried forward by a relatively few people.

The first of these—or the first of whom we have any knowledge—was John Julius Angerstein. The son of a German family who had emigrated to Russia, he was born in St Petersburg in 1735. Sent to London at the age of fourteen, he had served his apprenticeship in the counting house of a merchant—presumably a friend of his father's—who dealt with Russia. From there he had moved to Lloyd's where he had found his true *métier* in the world of marine insurance.

When you look at the portrait of Angerstein which hangs at Lloyd's today, you have the sense of a natural aristocrat of commerce. There is shrewdness in the face, worldliness and a certain disdain. It is not exactly arrogant, but you feel that it is not the face of a man who would have suffered fools gladly. If he had little time for fools, he had still less for knaves. Once, many years later, he was questioned about the presence in the Room of some unsavoury underwriters' clerks who were in the habit of writing risks on which they had no money to pay losses.

'I cannot speak to it,' said Angerstein with weary disdain. 'I do not know their names.' One senses a contempt which was not only on moral grounds. The wider contempt was for those who did not see Lloyd's, as he did, as a great instrument of commerce.

Angerstein was chairman of Lloyd's from 1790 to 1796, and in those days he was a nationally known figure, both as the financial adviser to William Pitt and as a patron of the arts whose private collection would later become the nucleus of the National Gallery.

Long before he became Chairman, it is safe to assume, he had been a dominating figure. Slips on which he had written a line were known as Julians, after his second Christian name. Angerstein gave a lead, the rest of the market would follow—just as more than a century later, when non-marine insurance began, the market would follow C. E. Heath.

As a broker, Angerstein placed the largest insurance then ever written at Lloyd's, for £656,800 on the treasure carried from Vera Cruz to England on a frigate called the *Diana*. Often he dealt in risks which must have at the time seemed both frightening and novel. In 1794, Lloyd's underwriters lost hundreds of thousands of pounds on Dutch and Russian ships seized by hostile governments in the Napoleonic War. Angerstein, quick to try to convert a huge loss to a potential profit, bought the salvage rights. 'Two years afterwards,' writes Gibb,

Lloyd's Coffee Rooms at the Royal Exchange in 1798

Replica of the 17th century coffee house in the Visitors' Gallery and Exhibition

John Julius Angerstein: the portrait by Sir Thomas Lawrence

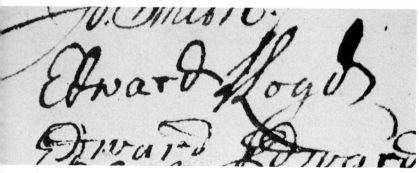

Edward Lloyd's signature

'the losses were repaid to underwriters and Angerstein's speculation proved profitable. (It was) the first recorded case of an underwriter speculating on the prospects of salvage after payment of a total loss!'

But in 1773 all this was in the future. At the time of his visit to the Mercers' Company Angerstein was only thirty-eight, an insurance broker with an office of his own in Old Broad Street.

From all the records it seems that the attempt to get the Royal Exchange rooms was his own idea. Angerstein had been one of the group which had originally headed the move to Pope's Head Alley, but at this stage he was not even a member of the newly formed Lloyd's Committee.

To a young man bursting with initiative and the sort of ranging far-sightedness which is part of his legacy to Lloyd's, the procrastinations of the Committee may well have been irritating. One can imagine his getting to hear of the two rooms 'late in lease to the British Fishery' and deciding to do something about it. At any rate, he seems to have taken matters into his own hands. He called a meeting of the members of Lloyd's, got their authority to proceed, and negotiated the lease of the rooms in his own name. On 16 November 1773 he and three other subscribers signed it 'for themselves and the rest of the Committee for New Lloyd's Coffee House' for twenty-one years at a rent of £160 a year.

Like the move to Pope's Head Alley, this second move to the Royal Exchange was much more than simply a change of location. In a particular sense it meant—and it is a point that seems worth saluting—the end of the coffee house. For three-quarters of a century marine insurance in London had been tied to the idea of the coffee house. Miraculously, it had survived and prospered. When one comes to think of it, it is a little as if cricket had survived because of the existence of the Tavern at Lord's or as if Eton had only kept going because of its tuck shop.

It was a debt of which Angerstein and his fellow members were well aware. Even when the Lloyd's market opened for the first time at the Royal Exchange on 5 March 1774, the main rooms were described as 'Coffee Rooms', and indeed coffee continued to be served in them. There were regulations about no sedan chairs being brought in. One innovation was a Loss and Arrival Book exhibited in the subscribers' room, which was kept for the members only, and was guarded by one of the waiters. Otherwise the scenery was much the same. There was still the pulpit which the Kidney would mount to declaim important news. The boxes were ranged round the walls in much the same way as they had been in Lombard Street.

One other point was significant. Just before the move from Pope's Head Alley the subscribers came to an arrangement with Thomas Fielding who had been, you may remember, Master of the coffee house in Pope's Head Alley. It was arranged that Fielding should go with them to the Royal Exchange, and should take his head waiter, Thomas Taylor, into partnership. Fielding and Taylor were to take the profits from the sale of coffee, and there were various arrangements made by the subscribers for payments to be made to Fielding's wife in the event of his death.

In other words the masters were now the servants. The underwriters and brokers were no longer mere frequenters of a coffee house.

They were now the subscribers of Lloyd's, and what they had achieved was the ground-plan of the modern market.

3
Unlimited Liability

'IT's very nice to welcome you here.'

'It's very nice to be here.'

'We'd just like to ask you,' says the chairman of the Rota Committee, 'one or two questions. We are here as representatives of the Council of Lloyd's. We'd like to make certain of one or two things.'

The candidate, who happens to be Irish, nods and says he quite understands. As well he might, for over the last few weeks he will have been carefully briefed about this meeting. The object of the Rota Committee is to make a final check on the credentials of anyone who is applying to join a syndicate—to become what is known at Lloyd's, a little mysteriously, as a Name.

'We'd like to be quite sure you've had things explained to you.' The chairman is in his middle forties, a quiet, courteous man with an air of authority which he tends to play down. 'You know what is meant by Unlimited Liability?'

The candidate nods, rather seriously this time, and says he does understand.

'We like to make sure about that. Down to your last shirt button.' The chairman grins amiably. So do the rest of the three-man committee. Unlimited Liability is something Lloyd's men like making jokes about, rather in the same way it is said that only really religious people can make jokes about God.

'And you've also understood about the control of your funds being in the hands of your underwriting agent? The point is it can make life rather difficult for an underwriter if he feels you're breathing down his neck.'

The Irishman says he can quite see that, and the underwriting agent who is here as his sponsor nods. If he hadn't explained that to his candidate, he says, he wouldn't have been doing his job very well. There is another general laugh. All the same, the Irishman looks round the room with a certain awe. With its chandeliers and Adam fireplace, the Council Room of Lloyd's must be one of the most spectacular rooms in London. The candidate has flown over for this meeting especially from Dublin, and you feel it is an important day for him, a bit like being taken to a new school by your parents.

'And you've read the terms of the agreement between you and the underwriting agent?' After this comes a few more general questions about whether the candidate has altered his financial arrangements since he completed his application. Everything seems to be in order, and the chairman looks up.

'Well. I think that's all we want to ask you. Was there anything you want to ask us?'

It seems the Irishman has no questions; the chairman shuffles his papers and looks up. 'Thank you *very* much. I do hope all goes well for you.' The expression sounds not merely formal—you feel he really likes the candidate and hopes he will succeed. The Irishman thanks them and goes out, then the mahogany door opens again.

This time they all get up—the candidate is a girl in her thirties, an attractive blonde in a red coat. There is an atmosphere of restrained gallantry—though Lloyd's has been admitting women for the last seventeen years, for the Committee, you feel, the experience is still novel.

After the chairman has done the initial courtesies they sit down. 'Mrs March, isn't it? I believe you've come up from Surrey today?'

Mrs March says she has, and the chairman says he hopes the weather wasn't too bad. They'd had somebody else from Surrey who had got stuck on the motorway because of the weather. Mrs March says that must have been the other side of the county, for her drive had been all right.

'Oh, that's good.' The chairman seems really relieved, then gets down to looking at her papers. 'Now the proposal here is that you're going to write £30,000 non-marine business with the Heath syndicate. And on the marine side up to £20,000 with Chester's. Have you met the underwriters who'll be handling your money?'

Mrs March says that she has just had lunch with them, and they were charming.

'I think that's very important.' The chairman nods approvingly. 'After all, they've got your underwriting fate under their pens.'

Next comes the question about Unlimited Liability. Mrs March says she'd been told what it means and she understands it.

'It's not a thing to be taken lightly,' says the chairman. 'We like to make sure you understand what it means. The only things you really need to know about Lloyd's,' he says, and everybody laughs, 'are Unlimited Liability and the Lutine Bell.'

There are a few more questions, then they get up. Lloyd's has demonstrated, if further demonstration were needed, its sense of style. Afterwards the chairman says to me that it's not always easy to keep the right balance between the dignified and the informal, but they do their best. 'We like to make it an occasion people can remember,' he says. 'So much of life is retrospect or looking forward. It's good to recognize a moment that means something.'

Beyond this, what has also been demonstrated is Lloyd's huge integrity. But what really is Unlimited Liability, and how does it work?

Lloyd's concern with its own history is not merely narcissistic. Almost everything you see in the modern market is the result of a long, slow process. What has been built up over 300 years is not simply the practice of how it works, but a set of principles. At the heart of these lies Unlimited Liability—the underwriter's obligation to pay on his losses.

In 1720, you remember, the private insurers of London were made personally liable for everything they had guaranteed to an assured person—the whole of their accumulated premiums, the law said, were to be made available to meet his claims. Over the years the principle had not always worked. Through the eighteenth century there had been many cases of underwriters failing to pay up.

On the other hand there had been instances—and they must have seemed remarkable in the free-for-all financial climate of those days—when the underwriters paid a claim as a matter of principle rather than because the law made them do so. In 1811 Angerstein could say of the underwriters at Lloyd's:

I have known them to pay a loss where the merchant has made a mistake, and called it ship instead of goods, or goods instead of ship, and the underwriter, knowing it, took no advantage, and paid the loss; these are facts from my books. I have known a ship insured from one place to Europe, when she came from another, and that has been paid . . .

But this did not mean there was any absolute guarantee that the underwriter would pay up. He was bound to do so by law, and if he was an honest man he was also bound by honour. But there were many loopholes, and the Committee of Lloyd's had not, as yet, the power to close them.

According to Gibb, even by 1850:

an underwriting member could fail to pay his liabilities, could make a compo-
sition with his creditors, could even pass through the bankruptcy court, and
still use the Room for broking and underwriting without any interference from
the Committee. The Committee had no power to act, and its only course in
dealing with a broken-down underwriter was to tell the door-keeper not to let
the man pass the barrier . . . If any insolvent underwriter had had the physical
strength to barge through the barricade or the moral determination to take
action at law against the Committee, nothing apparently could have prevented
him from continuing to subscribe any policy that was offered to him.

But gradually, through those middle years of the nineteenth century,
things were beginning to alter. In 1851 the Committee passed a bye-
law that if a member became bankrupt he should be expelled from
Lloyd's. Six years later, almost by chance, they accepted the first
deposit against insolvency made by a new member.

True, the deposit was not sought by the Committee. It seems to
have arisen simply because a certain Mr Sharp wanted to make his son
an underwriting member and in those days it was conventional for the
sponsor to guarantee that the person he was introducing would pay his
debts. For some reason Mr Sharp had an objection on principle to giving such a guarantee. He asked the Committee if they would, instead,
accept a deposit of £5,000 to meet any debts that his son might incur.

The Committee at Lloyd's do not seem to have regarded Mr
Sharp's idea as particularly important, but they accepted it, and the
acceptance became a precedent. By the beginning of the 1860s,
though there was still no rule about it, anyone becoming an underwriting member of Lloyd's produced a deposit. By 1866 the process had
become ratified—in cases where the Committee required a cash
deposit, there had to be a Deed of Trust.

Even now, the Committee were still far from seeing themselves as in
any way responsible for an underwriter's actions. In 1855, an underwriter named Gibson went bankrupt, and one of his creditors in Liverpool wrote to the Committee to ask them if they would see that a claim
on his syndicate was paid. The Committee replied that they had no
power to interfere. It was not in their province, they said, to discuss the
subject; they were 'simply a Committee for managing the affairs of the
establishment of Lloyd's'.

In other words, the process was not complete—there were still gaps
in the net of total security which Lloyd's was gradually weaving. The
old tradition was still that it was a broker's job to distinguish between

an underwriter who would pay his claims and an underwriter who would not. If he failed the Committee could now exclude him from the Room. But the Committee were not responsible beyond that, and so the situation went on till the end of the century. Then quite suddenly in 1903 something happened to change it. An underwriter named Burnand failed badly. The cause of his failure was that he had been running a travel agency as well as an underwriting syndicate.

Among other things Burnand had invested heavily in selling seats for the Coronation of King Edward VII. The Coronation had been postponed because of the King's illness, and the travel agency had lost its money. In an attempt to prop it up, he borrowed money from the banks, on the guarantee that his underwriting syndicate would insure the travel agency against any failure to meet their bills. What he had done, in effect, was to make his names responsible for debts amounting to £100,000, though most of them knew nothing about it.

In the event, Burnand himself was jailed, and four of his names were ruined. The incident was a storm signal for Lloyd's, but it was not the only one. In another case, an underwriter had borrowed money for his deposit from a friend, and paid his friend back from the premiums earned, so that when the claims came in there was no money to pay them.

Clearly the reputation of Lloyd's demanded some sort of action by the Committee. But given the nature of Lloyd's, what sort of action could they take? The whole point of Lloyd's as an insurance market had always been that it was not a company, but a collection of individuals. On the other hand, what was clearly needed was some form of direct control by the Committee. Slowly, and after much argument, they began to evolve the idea which was to become the corner-stone of their reputation in the twentieth century.

Put very simply, the idea was in two parts. First there would have to be what could be called a Premium Trust Fund, approved by the Committee, in which underwriters would be compelled to place their premiums. In this way no underwriter could take his profits until he knew what claims were going to be made against him. At the end of a set period he would be able to take the profits, but by then he would have lodged further premiums—there would consequently be a balance in the Trust Fund. Meanwhile the profits would have to be certified by the Committee of Lloyd's before any shares in them could be handed out to the names.

But the idea of certifying the profits implied something else—and the something else, in terms of Lloyd's history, was a revolution. It implied that the Committee would have to see the books of each underwriting syndicate, would have to act, in fact, as an auditor. In 1908 Lloyd's appointed a special committee to examine the possibility of setting up a new checking system.

From the beginning this was designed as far more than a mere accounting procedure. The Audit, as it began to be called, was designed to detect, at the first possible moment, any weakness in the financial structure of a syndicate. It would have the power to set a limit on the volume of business that any underwriter might write, according to the capital provided by his names.

Not surprisingly, the idea was not entirely acceptable to all the Edwardian individualists of Lloyd's; in November 1908 there was still doubt whether the procedure which the special committee had drawn up would be agreed to. But in 1908, as 150 years earlier, Lloyd's had its men of vision.

Just as Angerstein and his friends had seen the need to break clear of the gambling underwriters in the 1760s, so there was now a group of leading underwriters who saw what needed to be done. Prominent among them was Cuthbert Heath, the man who, in the 1880s, had written Lloyd's first non-marine insurance policy. Among the most treasured possessions of Lloyd's today is a piece of foolscap paper on which forty-two of its leading underwriters had signed their names to a few words in Heath's handwriting: 'We the undersigned underwriting Members, would agree to hand in to the Committee of Lloyd's annually a statement signed by an approved accountant that we were in possession of assets reasonably sufficient to wind up our underwriting accounts.'

For a scrap of paper, its influence was to be immense. Once Heath and the other leaders had come out in favour of it, the issue was no longer in doubt.

By March 1909 the members of Lloyd's submitted themselves to the Annual Audit for the first time, and the modern history of Lloyd's had begun.

With the coming of the Audit the Committee of Lloyd's assumed a new role. Without interference in the actual running of individual syndicates, they had now set up a means of control whose object was to protect the public and preserve Lloyd's reputation. Even so, as events were to show, they had not yet gone far enough.

It is one of the striking things about the story of Lloyd's that when-

ever there has been trouble it has always been followed by a deft move
to put Lloyd's house in order. When Angerstein and his friends saw
the reputation of the coffee house threatened by the gambling underwriters of the 1760s, they took rapid action to shed them. When the
Committee saw how Burnand had found it possible to convert his
names' money, they invented the Premium Trust Fund and the Audit.

In 1923 the Committee found themselves in similar, but much
worse, trouble. This time it was caused by an underwriter named
Harrison, whose business was in the non-marine market, and who
specialized in motor insurance. Among his clients were several companies involved in the then novel business of selling cars on hire
purchase.

In order to provide working capital for themselves, the hire-
purchase companies borrowed money from discount houses. The
security they offered was in the form of bills signed by the hire-
purchasers. Thus, if someone failed to complete his payments, the bill
meant that there would be at least a second-hand car to dispose of. If
the bills were also covered by an insurance policy which guaranteed
credit of the purchaser, it made the deal that much more solid-looking
from the point of view of the discount houses who were going to lend
the money.

Increasingly, Harrison began to deal in this kind of insurance—
credit insurance, as it is known. By early 1923 he had guaranteed more
than £2 million worth of bills, often knowing nothing of the true state
of credit of the person they were drawn on.

It was not long before there came the first ominous sound of Harrison's impending crash. One of his credit risks was a man named
Holsteinson, a Swedish citizen living in London, whose business was
owning fleets of coaches and taxis. At least he claimed to own them—
probably some at least of the taxis and coaches were real. The rest was
imaginary. Holsteinson had invented registrations and engine
numbers, on the strength of which the optimistic Harrison had guaranteed his bills of credit. Some time during the spring of 1923
Holsteinson disappeared.

Harrison found himself owing the discount brokers £17,000 on a
fleet of fictitious taxis.

It is conceivable that if Harrison had admitted his follies to the
Committee of Lloyd's, the result would have been no worse than a ban
on his future underwriting. But there was something else which Harrison could not admit to the Committee. This was that he had been

keeping two sets of books, one which he submitted to the Audit, and another which reported his true dealings.

All that summer Harrison went on writing more and more policies in a blind attempt to extricate himself from his troubles. Meanwhile the Audit sub-committee had begun to scent something wrong. They had already asked for more money to be paid into his names' Trust Funds. Then, in October 1923, the bank refused to honour one of his cheques. Harrison was asked to produce his true accounts to the Chairman of Lloyd's, A. L. Sturge. When Sturge examined them, he found the amount owing to the discount brokers was in the region of £200,000.

The importance of the Harrison case lies not in the re-telling of the story of a pathetic fraud, but in what followed. Within eight days of Harrison's confession, Sturge had been through the books, called a meeting of the Committee and laid the facts before them.

When they understood the situation, Sturge said one thing to them, and what he said was historic. He told them that Harrison's debts would have to be met by the other members of Lloyd's. He had no authority to say it, and that in a sense makes what he told them more impressive. It was the expression, perhaps the most complete expression, of Lloyd's integrity.

Before the Committee meeting broke up on that October afternoon, Sturge's view had been accepted. Harrison's debts were to be charged on every member of Lloyd's, in proportion to their premium income. When the underwriters paid their shares, the amount varied from £10,000 to eightpence. The members of Lloyd's had not only demonstrated the truth of the old description that individually they were underwriters but collectively they were Lloyd's—they had given it a new force. From 1923 onwards, a Lloyd's policy carried a guarantee of liability far beyond that which any conventional insurance company has ever offered; greater indeed, than some conventional insurance companies offer to this day.

It remained to secure the last loopholes. Soon after the Harrison case, the whole hazardous field of credit insurance was completely barred by the Committee of Lloyd's. In 1924 it became compulsory for all policies to be issued through the Policy Signing Office, which would bring a new means of tighter control. An additional fund called the Central Fund was set up to cover any possible future defaults by an underwriter who might find a means, as Harrison had done, to cheat the Audit, or for that matter an underwriter who quite genuinely could not pay his debts. This fund—it has now risen to nearly £300 million according to the most recent figures—was to be made up from contributions from all members of Lloyd's, in proportion to their premium income.

Thus the safety net was now complete, and the principle of Unlimited Liability established. How does this affect the individual underwriter today? It is time now to look at what an underwriter really does, and what we mean by a syndicate.

One of the things they are fond of quoting at Lloyd's is an Elizabethan definition of insurance—'by means of whiche it comethe to passe that upon the losse or perishinge of any shippe there followethe not the undoinge of any man, but the losse lighteth reather easilie upon many than heavilie upon few.'

Obviously this principle of spreading the load works in the sense of various underwriters taking a line or percentage on a risk. On what is always called the hull of a ship or a jet aircraft, for instance, even the most heavily involved underwriter will usually take only about seven per cent.

But this is only the first stage of spreading the load. Obviously not all the seven per cent is the underwriter's own money. He writes his line as representative of a syndicate. There are about 365 syndicates in the Room of Lloyd's—128 marine, 150 non-marine, and about forty each for motor insurance and aviation. Mrs March, you remember, was going to write her marine insurance with Chester's. Thinking it might be useful to see who was actually going to be handling her money, I rang up Henry Chester and explained that I was writing a book about Lloyd's and asked if we could meet and have a talk.

Henry Chester said he'd be delighted. He and the leading underwriter on his syndicate met most mornings for coffee at 10.15. If I'd like to come along and join them, I could learn something about the syndicate and how it fitted in the general picture.

I had learnt meanwhile that Henry Chester is highly regarded at Lloyd's as one of its elder statesmen. He has been in the market since the end of the war. As a leading marine underwriter he was an influential figure in the creation of the oil-rig market in the 1960s, and as a member of the Committee helped to steer Lloyd's through the troubled period of the early 1980s. A dark, serious-looking man with a trenchant way of talking and a slightly brooding kind of deadpan humour, he has now retired from active underwriting, but still comes to the office most days.

To meet him I went to his office on the eighth floor, which has a fine sweeping view from the Monument to Highgate Hill. An adjoining office looks over the Room itself, where the Chester syndicate has a grid position close to the Lutine Bell.

He began by explaining that, to put it simply, Chester's was really two firms. 'H. G. Chester and Co. is the underwriting agency. A. H. Chester and Others is the syndicate—the others being the names on whose behalf we write risks.' H. G. Chester and Co., he explained, had been started by his uncle, who came to the market in 1903, and had begun by writing marine risks for a syndicate of ten names. Among the ships he had insured had been the *Titanic*. In the outer office they still had the entry relating to her in the loss book, if I'd like to see it.

He rang the bell and asked one of his secretaries to bring the book, and he looked up 14 April, 1912 and ran his finger down five sets of figures, written with a scratch pen in handwriting that had gone a gingery colour with time. 'That's my uncle's handwriting,' said Henry Chester. '£542 on jewellery, £5,000 on the hull to the brokers. Two additional lines to other brokers. We must have lost more than £8,000 on her. That was a lot of money in 1912.'

He closed the file and put it back, going on to say that his uncle had been a fine underwriter, much respected in the market, and a man who had really loved ships. In his later years he had been a great benefactor to the Methodist Church, in which Henry Chester himself was also brought up. He wasn't sure whether he was still a Methodist, but some of the principles had stuck; for example, he had never written arms or ammunition.

At that point we were joined by Geoffrey Welch, followed by one of the secretaries bringing in the morning coffee. As in Edward Lloyd's time, most people in the market begin the day with several cups of coffee, either in their offices or in the Captain's Room, whose name dates from the days when sea-captains would come in wearing their seaboots to meet their underwriters over mutton chops and claret.

Geoffrey Welch, a spruce, shrewd-looking man, is the 'active' underwriter. This means he is responsible for all that happens at the box. Assisting him, he said, were two other underwriters, who specialized in hull and cargo.

What sort of things, I asked, would they normally discuss at this morning meeting? Geoffrey Welch said it depended, which Lloyd's

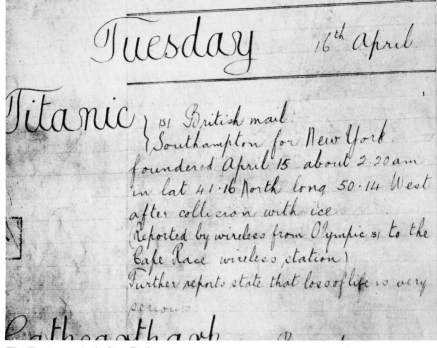

The *Titanic* entry in the Loss Book

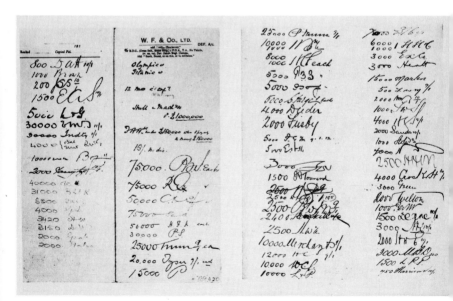

The *Titanic* slip: the figures represent each underwriter's line, with his initial next to it

In 1985 Peter Miller became the first Chairman of Lloyd's to visit China: he is pictured here with Tien Jiyun

The Royal Exchange around 1890. Lloyd's returned there in 1844, after the original building was burnt down in 1838

men are fond of saying, as if they rather pride themselves that nothing is done purely by the rules. Sometimes they might just talk about last night's programme on the telly. Another time it might be a question of deciding whether or not the syndicate should pull out of some unprofitable type of business. Since they had mentioned hull and cargo, I asked if that was the main type of business that the box writes.

'It would have been, thirty years ago,' said Geoffrey Welch. 'But not now. It's between thirty and forty per cent today. Marine underwriters used to rely on hull and cargo, plus some odds and ends. Now it's the odds and ends that make up the main part.'

'What are the odds and ends?'

He sipped his coffee and said it was a mixture. 'War risks. Confiscations. Rig business in the North Sea. A few non-marine risks. And excess-of-loss.' This, he explained, was reinsurance. An excess-of-loss policy is the means by which an insurance company or a Lloyd's syndicate will lay off a proportion of its own risk.

I asked why the hull and cargo business had gone down, and Mr Welch said that basically it was because of the world recession in shipping. 'Nowadays even the Greek fleets are a lot smaller than they were. The only really big fleets are in the Far East.' But cargo included some risks that I might find interesting. I might, he suggested, go down to the box and have a chat to Jim Bragg, the cargo underwriter, later.

I turned to war risks—on that particular morning there had been another Iraqi attack on a tanker in the Persian Gulf. Did such things make an underwriter lose sleep?

'If you were going to lose sleep, you'd get no sleep at all,' Geoffrey Welch said rather drily. 'When you write a hundred risks a day, which one are you going to worry over?' Henry Chester observed that in something like the Gulf war-zone, you had comparatively few risks at any one time, but that they were all of them in danger. 'So, you get no spread of risk, which is what underwriters look for.'

Geoffrey Welch looked up a bit lugubriously and mentioned that there was now a new system of getting oil out of the Gulf. 'They bring it out from Kharg Island on a shuttle-service to the other tankers. The other day I was asked to quote for the shuttle, one trip, one way. I quoted thirty-two and a half per cent.'

Henry Chester asked if he had got the order. Geoffrey Welch said he hadn't, and they both laughed. Was that, I asked, an example of what they would call a bad risk.

Geoffrey Welch deliberated. 'I don't think there's such a thing as a bad risk. There's a cheap risk, but not a bad risk. There's a price for almost anything, and if you can get that price, you write it. I suppose if it came down to it, I'd write something really terrible, like glass bottles on deck. You'd have to charge about forty per cent. But if you can get the right rate, then you'd write it.'

After a while Geoffrey Welch thought it was time for him to be at the box, and Henry suggested we went back to the question of how the syndicate fitted in with the agency. 'You're really dealing with two things, a syndicate of underwriters with unlimited liability. And an underwriting agency, which is a limited liability company,' he said, getting out a large volume called *Lloyd's Underwriting Syndicates* which he placed on the desk. 'If you look in here, you'll find the names of the syndicate and the agency occurring about seventy times between them. The main reference is to H. G. Chester and Company Ltd which is the agency for our syndicate. The next lot of references are to sub-agents who place names on our syndicate and vice versa. Most names are on at least four syndicates, the one they basically join, but also several others. For example, our syndicate doesn't write fire or motor business. If one of our names decides to write those classes, we place him with a fire or motor syndicate, acting as a sub-agent. The lady you saw at the Rota Committee was joining a non-marine syndicate—but she wanted to spread her risk over marine as well, so she came to us for those risks. Our own syndicate actually consists of 250 names, plus another 2,500 from other agents.'

I said I thought I'd got that, and we went on to look at the list of names on Chester's own syndicate. Opposite each name was written a figure, for example 20 or 100. Each of these, Henry Chester said, represented £1,000—thus the person with 20 opposite his name was prepared to write up to £20,000.

Before anyone can be a name at Lloyd's, he went on to explain, he now has to pass a means test. This means he has to show the Committee of Lloyd's that he has a minimum of £100,000 in capital. The amount of premium a name is allowed to write can never exceed 250 per cent of his capital. Each name has to make a deposit with the Corporation of Lloyd's equal to twenty per cent of his agreed premium limits. If a name with means of £100,000 writes a premium of £250,000, his required deposit would be £50,000.

Then where, I asked, did unlimited liability come in? If the underwriter made a heavy loss, didn't the name just lose his deposit?

'Not at all, that's the whole point. It's not just like buying shares on the Stock Market. If you have shares in a company and it goes bust, you lose your money. If you put your money in a Lloyd's syndicate and it goes bust, you could lose everything. First of all the Committee of Lloyd's will take all the money you've got in your underwriting account at the moment. If that isn't enough they'll take your bank account. Finally they'll take your deposit.' In theory, he went on, they talk about the shirt off your back, and in the past there had always been a few worrying cases where people had had to sell their house and move into a bungalow. Then, in the late 1970s and early 1980s, Lloyd's had hit a wave of trouble. There had been severe losses over asbestosis and computer leasing. Worse still had been the various underwriting scandals which had landed a lot of people in trouble.* None of his own names had lost money on them, because he'd been fortunate enough not to have any names on those syndicates. The only time his own syndicate had lost money had been in the late 1960s when there had been a bit of a trough anyway, and then there had come a couple of American hurricanes to clinch it—Hurricane Betsy had gone right up the Mississippi and ripped into a whole lot of ships that the syndicate had written. In those two years the syndicate hadn't sent the names their annual cheque—it had to ask them each for £4,000. He himself had lost £24,000 though mostly not on his own syndicate. 'It wasn't exactly the moment I'd have chosen, because we'd got kids at school and there was a credit squeeze on. All the same, we stood it.'

It occurred to me that an underwriter must do pretty well the rest of the time to face up to losses like these, and he agreed. 'If you've got the cash to start with and you have got the right underwriting agent, you can do very nicely—anyone writing up to £100,000 can make £10,000 in a year. You're allowed to write a multiple of your deposit, and you're using the money twice—because the Committee of Lloyd's don't invest your deposit for themselves, they pay you the dividend. Even so it's the worst thing in the world for a worrier. We do occasionally get the sort of name who will hear that some ship's gone down, and they'll ring up to see if we've had a line on it. On the whole, though, they're a minority—the names leave us to get on with it, and it's important that they do. I always tell the new names, when they join, to remember that the underwriter's in there with them too. It's a bit like trusting the captain of an aircraft.'

What, I asked, was the real skill of underwriting? Henry Chester

* See p. 81.

thought for a bit and said it was a mistake to suppose, as most people did, that the worst thing that could happen to an underwriter was a shipwreck or an earthquake: in a sense, he said, they thrived on trouble. If there was a loss, it meant they would simply put the rates up. 'If you've done your sums right, you wouldn't be affected by the loss of a North Sea drilling platform. It'd make a hole in your profits but it wouldn't worry you. Where you do go wrong is when your premium levels are wrong.'

(Later I asked another underwriter the same question and he said it was a bit like being a racing driver. He quoted the example of Fangio, who was said to have calculated the exact speed that was right for every racetrack. 'He'd decide on his speed for the course and stick to it, whatever happened to everyone else. If he'd got his speed right he'd overtake people who were too slow and the people who tried to go round faster would blow up. In the same way if you get your premium-rate right, you won't be hit by losses.')

Coming back to the syndicate, I enquired what would happen if somebody wanted to become an underwriter and he didn't happen to have £100,000 lying around?

Henry Chester stressed that Lloyd's was nowadays much more democratic. His own guess was that about half the underwriters nowadays had come up from being clerks in the Room. In this case, the syndicates that employ them would put up the deposits. On Henry Chester's box there are seventeen people including the three underwriters, and seven of them are members. In the case of a Lloyd's man, the deposit is reduced to £25,000 and there is no means test. 'From the syndicate's point of view,' he said, 'it's worth it because it repays their loyalty.'

Just now, he said, he was working on the syndicate's 1983 account. Lloyd's results are always announced three years in arrears, to allow leeway for what are known as 'long-tail' claims. 'We know the premiums and claims at the end of thirty-six months. What I'm having to do is to calculate the appropriate reserves we need to meet any claims which may come in later.' Before the accounts were completed, all the figures, he explained, have to be checked and approved by an approved firm of Lloyd's auditors. The figures have to be reported to Lloyd's which also checks continually to ensure that the syndicates and the individual names do not exceed their approved premium limits.

I could see that Henry Chester needed to get on with his accounts, so I put my notebook away and began to move off. He walked with me as far as the gallery which looks down on the vast space of the new Room. Not all the older generation of underwriters were quite sure they approved of it, but Henry Chester thought it was the best thing that had happened to the market in a long time. 'I think it's fabulous, the sign of Lloyd's confidence in the future. I went down to the box last week, and wrote a risk. Just to say I'd written in the new Room.'

Lloyd's present tally of 31,000 names would have startled earlier underwriters. In the 1890s, according to Lloyd's historian D. E. W. Gibb, half a dozen names on a syndicate was thought a 'dangerously large' number. Even by the 1950s, the number had risen only to 4,000 and it was not until 1968, when the Cromer report suggested that the market needed to increase its capacity, that the names proliferated. First foreign, then women, members were admitted, though Lloyd's rejected Cromer's proposal that companies might become names. A limited liability company, the Committee felt, could hardly be subject to the unlimited liability that Lloyd's insists upon.

What sort of people are Lloyd's names today? After I had left Henry Chester I had a look at the members' book where all the 31,000 names are listed. In the course of about a quarter of an hour's browsing, I came across four members of the Royal Family—Princess Michael is the latest—several judges, and a clutch of jockeys. In Parliament, Edward Heath and John Wakeham are both names, along with a few dozen other Tory MPs. Membership of Lloyd's is the only outside interest apart from farming that a Cabinet Minister does not have to give up but he may not actually underwrite or receive any profits during his period in office. Stockbrokers used not to be allowed to become names, because of the possible liabilities of their own business, but are now admitted if it can be shown there is no clash of interest.

Apart from John Julius Norwich and Melvyn Bragg, literature and the arts are not strongly represented. But actress Susan Hampshire is there, and so is her theatrical-impresario-shipowner husband Eddie Kulukundis, who is a member of the Council. There are fewer pop stars than you might expect, though Dave Gilmour of Pink Floyd, Andy Fletcher of Depeche Mode and Adam Ant are there. Sport is rather stronger than the arts, with Trevor Brooking, Colin Cowdrey, Mark Cox, Virginia Wade, ex-racing driver James Hunt and National Hunt jockey Johnny Francome. Apart from insurance men, the strongest group is peers, of which over 200 noble names are listed. On one syndicate alone I counted eight—but membership of Lloyd's is by no means an upper-class preserve. 'Twenty-five years ago,' I was told by an underwriter who serves on the Rota Committee, 'we'd have thought twice about someone who wasn't a gent. Nowadays that's all gone. You get some young chap who's built up a business from scratch, had it taken over and wants to make the money he's earned work for him. These are the sort of whizz-kids that Lloyd's today can do with.'

John Masefield would not find many British coasters butting through the Channel nowadays, but there are still most sorts of cargo. On the Chester box the list seemed to include everything from fine arts to fishmeal. Jim Bragg, the cargo underwriter, sits almost opposite the Lutine Bell—a shortish, sharpish man with a jaunty air, backchatting with a stream of brokers. The first had brought a large-scale risk for a famous firm of cable-makers. They were bidding for a £46m contract in Saudi Arabia, the broker said, and they wanted a preliminary idea of the cost of the insurance. Jim Bragg wanted to know the port of discharge for the cable, which turned out to be Jeddah.

'That's all right then. First-class roads.' He had been, he said, all over that coast. 'But I think we'll have to get someone to survey the discharge.'

'At your expense?'

'At their bloody expense,' said Jim Bragg mildly. 'It's no good having it all tied up at the UK port if it's going to get knocked about when it gets there.'

Eventually he told the broker he thought he might do it 0.50 per cent plus scale war. War risks are charged at a rate agreed by all the Lloyd's and company underwriters in the London market. The broker seemed happy to take this back to his client, and Jim Bragg moved on to a risk for corned beef going to Hamburg.

'Knowing you, I suppose the rates are low?'

The broker said politely that he had hoped Jim might be generous and do it for 0.5.

'0.75.' Jim Bragg picked up an old fashioned scratch pen and dipped it in his inkwell. 'This isn't another charity job,' he said, and the broker grinned back. Afterwards he explained that the previous day the same broker had come round with a policy for £15,000 worth of Christmas cards which a charity was sending to Australia to be sold there. Jim Bragg had written them for a nominal premium of £5. It was the sort of thing, he said, that made the market human.

Meanwhile, he had moved on from corned beef to the fine arts. The next slip was for an exhibition of mediaeval paintings that was being brought from America for a Bond Street exhibition. The policy had a limit of £1m any one item, with £15m any one location, meaning that the paintings would be covered both in transit and while they were on show. They would be brought from the USA on a date which would be told to no one but the leading underwriter.

The next broker in the queue had been waiting quite a long time. His slip was for a cargo of potatoes from Vlissingen to Seville. 'I don't write potatoes, sir,' Jim said rather kindly.

The broker did his best, but Jim was definite about it. 'No, sir, I'm sorry, I haven't written bagged potatoes for thirty years.' When the young man had moved off rather disconsolately, Jim told me the trouble was that the bags broke because they were knobbly and difficult to handle. One day years ago he had seen potatoes strewn all over a wharf near London Bridge and resolved that potatoes were a bad risk.

By now it was getting on for one o'clock, and most of the market was drifting off for lunch. Jim Bragg was in deep, quiet conversation with the next broker in his queue, so I put away my notebook, thinking it was time for me to make an exit. But just then Jim turned and said that I should not go for a moment. What he and the broker were talking about was a ship that had been hit by a missile in the Gulf while carrying 10,000 tons of crude oil. The cargo had remained intact, and arguably would have become underwriters' salvage if there was a claim. But, said the broker, the bad news was that the oil had been fraudulently sold off.

'Do we know these people?'

The broker said something rather delicate about believing they might have been involved in stolen cargoes in the past, and Jim's brow went a bit dark. 'My father used to say never put your foot in muddy water unless you put your sock on.'

The two of them went off to see if there was anything they could decide about it over lunch. On my way out, I decided to take in the fourth floor gallery from which visitors can overlook the Room, where you can see a replica of Lloyd's coffee-house and other exhibits ranging from pirate ships to a video of architect Richard Rogers explaining the design plan of the new Lloyd's building. I browsed for a while over these memories of Lloyd's past, listening to the taped sounds of storms and sea-shanties. Whether it was pirate brigs in the Caribbean or stolen oil-cargoes in the Gulf, it seemed things did not change much.

I wandered out of the exhibition and out to the huge windows that look across the City roofs towards Tower Bridge and the Pool of London. For a moment I had a picture of the forest of masts there had once been, of seventeenth-century sea captains walking up greasy steps to Edward Lloyd's coffee-house in Tower Street, and it occurred to me that at Lloyd's you never feel far from the sea. Other City offices sometimes seem to exist in a vacuum, a sort of artificial world of mining shares and cocoa futures without reference to the real world where people actually mine diamonds and plant cocoa.

At Lloyd's the ships are real, and it is part of the quality of the place.

Peter Miller welcomes HM the Queen to the New Lloyd's

PART TWO

The Modern Market

4
America Discovers Lloyd's

It often happens that a great innovator's chance comes at a time of crisis. It may be an art-form grown threadbare, an administration grown corrupt—it is the need for reform that makes the individual's opportunity. Lloyd's, in its nature, has always been a place for pioneers. Just as Angerstein had cleaned up the gambling market of the 1760s, so the opportunity came, over a century later, for the man who was to be the founder of the modern Lloyd's.

Perhaps it is not quite true to say that Lloyd's in the 1880s was in a state of crisis, but it was certainly in a period of down-swing. Business had begun to drift away to the big marine insurance companies. Lloyd's might still be a unique institution, but it was in danger of losing out to more outward-looking rivals.

Partly, perhaps, it had been a gentleman's occupation for too long. When one outstanding underwriter, F. W. Marten, moved into an expanding world market by writing enormous lines on his marine risks, the Room shook its collective head in horror. As far as non-marine business went, there were a few boxes where you could insure against fire risks, but that was all. Lloyd's, it seemed possible, could decay into a venerable institution inhabited by elderly gentlemen with distant memories of tea-clippers.

Such was Lloyd's when there arrived, in 1880, a shrewd, rather dapper-looking young man named Cuthbert Heath. The son of an admiral, he had been turned down for the navy. Possibly a psycho-analyst could make something of the fact. The essence of his contribution was that he steered Lloyd's away from what had been, till now, an almost total interest in marine matters.

Heath became an underwriting member in 1883, and almost immediately began writing what seemed to the market novel, if eccentric, business. Fire policies had existed before, but Heath invented a new sort which not merely covered a company against fire, but against the loss of business that followed. He wrote reinsurance for a company called the Hand-in-Hand, in which his father had an interest.

The more conservative-minded figures in the Captains' Room may have deplored such ideas, but there was nothing in Lloyd's rules to stop Heath's innovations. Soon afterwards he was asked if he would write the reinsurance for the American branch of another English company, and he did so. It was a landmark in the history of Lloyd's—the first American risk ever written in the non-marine market.

In 1887, Heath moved into another field which seemed startlingly new. In those days there was no such thing as an insurance against being burgled. One day a broker was insuring his own furniture against fire with Heath, and asked him, since the crime-rate was on the increase, if he'd mind insuring him against burglary too? Almost as a joke, Heath wrote it. Within two years the broker's firm was advertising that it could effect insurance at Lloyd's against theft and robbery, with or without violence.

Other innovations followed. One day a relative of Heath's lost a piece of jewellery which she had insured with him against theft. There was no cover for loss, he explained, but immediately saw a new opportunity—if you could insure against burglary, why not against losing your jewels as well? He went back to his box, thought the matter over, and came up with a premium-rate of ten shillings for each £100 of cover. It was not only the first form of insurance against loss, but the premium-rate stood for fifty years. Almost as a natural follow-up came the idea of insuring diamonds in transit.

Within a few years of Heath's arrival at Lloyd's the market was insuring things which, in the 1870s, would have been unheard of. They were insuring factories in Chicago and Baltimore against fire, they were insuring farmers in Southern Europe against hail damage. In 1901 came Lloyd's first motor insurance—even though it was written in the marine market, and the car was treated as a ship navigating on dry land. By the time Lloyd's wrote the first aviation policy in 1911 they had at least moved a little away from the marine image—the pilot was referred to as 'the driver'.

In all these new departures the prime mover had been Cuthbert Heath. 'His name is honoured today,' writes Gibb, 'not because he started non-marine underwriting at Lloyd's but because he revolutionised, both at Lloyds and elsewhere, the business of non-marine insurance and enormously widened the service he offered to the commercial world . . . Today whenever a man says that Lloyd's will insure anything, he is paying an . . . unconscious tribute to the genius of Cuthbert Heath.'

In the story of the modern Lloyd's two things stand out. One was Heath's invention of a non-marine market. The other was America's discovery of Lloyd's. The two events were not linked in the sense that one caused the other, but they were linked just the same. The point was that Lloyd's was doing the right thing at the right moment for the huge and expanding American market.

In the past there had been many links with America. Lloyd's agents had been appointed there since the beginning of the nineteenth century, and in 1840 a Chairman of Lloyd's had made a six months' tour of the United States, the first ever by a Chairman in office to a foreign country.

Even so the links had been formal ones, such as there might have been with any other trading country. (If you look at the index of Frederick Martin's *History of Lloyd's*, published in 1876, it is significant that you will find America mentioned only twice, and non-marine insurance not at all.)

But now, as the 1890s began, something completely different happened, and on a completely different scale. With her new and booming industries, America was of necessity insurance-minded. A new breed of capitalist was growing up, many of them immigrants who had started from nothing and had no resources to fall back on. Soon they were asking for more insurance than the home-grown industry could cope with. They began to look abroad to Europe, and they found Lloyd's. Of all the European insurers, nothing else quite matched their own individualistic approach.

What is important to notice, looking back, is that none of this could have happened without the newly-created non-marine market. The great commercial need of the booming America of the 1890s was cover for its new-found prosperity. If a Boston millionaire wanted insurance for anything from his factory to his mistress's jewels, he could get it at Lloyd's. An Illinois saloon-keeper could get cover at Lloyd's—and nowhere else—to protect him from the new law which said he was responsible for damage done by anyone who had got drunk in his saloon. The first American motor policy came in 1907, for $2,500 on the White steam car in Chicago. Across the whole booming, rip-roaring continent a new name was beginning to be known—the name of Lloyd's of London.

Indeed, it was becoming so well known that it was being borrowed. In 1910 there were 37 different insurance companies in New York alone, all trading, prosperously but unofficially, under the name of Lloyd's.

Ultimately the test of an insurer is whether he pays up, and on 6 April 1906 there took place one of the greatest natural disasters in the history of the world, and one which has ever since echoed through the history of Lloyd's and of insurance. At twelve minutes past five in the morning of that day, the fissure known to geologists as the San Andreas fault slipped over an area of 270 miles, shattering the city of San Francisco where, in the space of a single minute, 30,000 houses were destroyed, including nearly 500 city blocks. Seven hundred people were dead and over a quarter of a million homeless. In the insurance world the reverberations continued for months. If a building was covered for fire, some of the companies claimed, then the policy would not apply if the fire had been caused or preceded by an earthquake.

'More than a third of the San Francisco fire business,' wrote *The Times* in a cautious leader, 'is estimated to be in the hands of British offices, where the calculation of liability must be a matter of some anxiety.' On another page the paper's Berlin correspondent wrote that among the German companies, where many of the San Francisco risks had been insured, 'the view is expressed that where a building collapsed and then took fire, the insurance companies are not liable.'

In the event many, though not the British, companies did repudiate their liability. Lloyd's did not. The final claim on their underwriters was in the region of $100,000,000—a staggering figure for those days. It was, one might say, the moment of truth. Lloyd's had not merely survived it, but created a new and massive goodwill for the future.

From now on it would no longer be a market which primarily insured ships. Nor would its business be primarily British. The stress would be increasingly American, and increasingly on the non-marine side.

Today just on half of all Lloyd's business comes from the United States. How, when all countries operate laws to protect their domestic markets, does this work out in practice? In the United States insurers work under licence—in most towns you will find the agent, or representative, of the main insurance companies. 'If you want to place an insurance,' I was told by a partner in Lloyd's American attorneys, 'you go to an agent who is licensed under state law. In the early days the licensing authorities didn't know what to make of Lloyd's. It wasn't chauvinism—they were simply suspicious of the idea of a risk being placed with some distant insurer who wasn't subject to the local laws.'

Since then, insurance regulations have been adapted to admit Lloyd's. In two states, Illinois and Kentucky, Lloyd's is freely licensed. In other states, an agent may place insurance with Lloyd's only when he has exercised what the law calls 'due diligence' in trying to place the risk in the domestic market. The point is that when he *has* exercised due diligence he can go to Lloyd's—which in its nature and with its resources writes many kinds of insurance that the domestic companies do not. Again, the scale of a risk may often be so large that it cannot all be covered in the local market. In this case, too, the business is likely to come to Lloyd's.

Meanwhile what about the regulations in the two states where Lloyd's is licensed—Kentucky and, more significantly because of its huge industrial importance, Illinois? Here insurance can be placed direct: in Chicago it will go through the offices of Lord, Bissell and Brook, attorneys-at-law. Roughly having the same function as Lloyd's Policy Signing Office, the attorneys' role is to see that both state laws and Lloyd's own rules are complied with. 'The sort of thing we might get,' says John Smith, the attorney who looks after Lloyd's Illinois business, 'is a broker coming up with a tailored policy that turns out to be thinly veiled strike insurance. I'll have a look at it and it might raise questions in my mind as to whether it was against public policy, as laid down by the Illinois code, which says that an employer can't insure against his employees going on strike.' To take another example, the policy might be for financial guarantee insurance, which is permitted by the Illinois code but not at Lloyd's. In this case John Smith might also query, and if necessary, stop it.

Probably the most impressive symbol of Lloyd's trans-Atlantic link is the American Trust Fund. This had its origins in 1939, when American brokers became concerned as to what might happen to their claims on London underwriters if war broke out. Before 1939 it had been a common practice for underwriters to leave their premiums in the United States untouched. Since Britain had gone off the Gold Standard in 1931, it reduced exchange problems and gave confidence to American brokers.

Now, however, the situation was different. No American broker supposed that a Lloyd's underwriter would default; nor did they greatly fear the possibility that Britain would be overrun by the Nazis. What they did fear was that the British Government would impose restrictions on the international transfer of currencies. If that did happen, what were the chances of American claims being met?

There was only one possible answer, and it was both bold and far-reaching—that all American premiums should be paid into a separate account, to be held in the United States. Underwriters would receive their profits only after claims, or the possibility of claims, had been allowed for. The machinery was rapidly set up and in August 1939 the American Trust Fund opened with capital resources of $40 million. Today it stands at more than $6 billion.

If it neither flies nor floats, the non-marine market will insure it. You might almost add if it is American as well. The US business ranges from earthquakes and tornadoes to meat-packing stations in Chicago. There is the reinsurance of American doctors' schemes—known as the Bedpan Mutuals—which insure their members against the chance of removing some vital part from a patient who has hoped to merely have his big toe straightened. There are errors and omissions policies for lawyers who may get sued by their clients, or surveyors whose reports omit to mention dry-rot. There are petro-chemical plants and fair-grounds, everything from libel to violinists' hands and baseball teams, which cost underwriters a lot of money when they went on strike a few years back.

I went and sat on Box 222, home of the Frank Barber syndicate. Malcolm Cox, the underwriter, is a highly professional young man with plenty of the deadpan humour which underwriters favour. He sat in front of one of the video screens on which he can instantly call up the track-record of a risk brought by a broker. He had positioned it, he said, so the broker beside him could only see an empty green screen.

This was put to the test when a broker came along, craning his neck to try to see the figures.

'Don't try to look at my screen.'

'I was only looking to see if it was working.'

'It's broker-proof. Only the righteous can look at my screen.'

Malcolm Cox is young, like everyone else on the Barber box. They work as a team, he said, going to tea and coffee together. 'Living and working so close, you have to accept the possibility of getting on each other's nerves, but so far it hasn't happened. We expect people to work hard, but we're not averse to the odd joke.'

Another broker came up with the reinsurance of a mutual scheme set up by Florida housebuilders to cover themselves for damage caused by major windstorms. Lloyd's has specialized in this type of insurance since the days of Heath, who based his own rates on his research into windstorm records and statistics going back 600 years. The premium on this one would have surprised Heath. In dollars, it was a quarter of a million.

'Do they give you any idea of the coastal exposure?' The Florida coast, Malcolm explained to me, could get up to twenty-five windstorms in any one year.

'It's spread through the whole of Florida,' said the broker, adding a bit less confidently that you had to look on the bright side.

'I'm not really looking for Florida. I don't think it's for me,' said Malcolm rather resolutely and the broker moved off.

The next slip was for an opencast coalmine on the American west coast. Malcolm tapped his keyboard. The screen announced that the total insurance was for $438m, covering five pits and a dragline which, he said, was what they use to get the coal out.

'The problem with draglines is always U and O.' This, it seemed, meant Use and Occupancy. If the dragline is damaged and there is difficulty in replacing it, the insurer might have to pay a relatively small property damage loss but many times more for business interruption. 'Do they keep spares?'

The broker produced a thick manual which listed various technical procedures, including what they did in times of flood or snowslide. The mine sounded a fairly inhospitable place, but after he and the broker had browsed over the manual for several minutes, Malcolm wrote 0.25 per cent, which still seemed like a lot of money. At any rate the broker went off cheerfully, to be followed in by an amiable character with a Gladstone bag, about five times the size of the usual broker's slipcase.

'You've got the biggest bag in the Room,' said Malcolm wonderingly. 'You're like a conjurer. Have you got a rabbit in there?' The contents turned out to be a stack of risks: householders and automobile covers from Quebec. Malcolm explained that these were written under what is called a binding authority, under which an appointed agent on the spot can write risks on behalf of the Barber syndicate—his own job now was to make a spot-check to see that they were all right.

The broker noticed Malcolm eyeing his watch. It was getting on for teatime, and the covers looked like an hour's work.

'Tell me to sod off when you've had enough,' said the broker cheerfully. 'But you're getting a quality book here.'

'I wish I could share your confidence.' All the same he stamped the first policy and put an initial on it.

'This next one you can just close your eyes and write.' After he had initialled a few more, Malcolm suggested that I wasn't going to spend my time very profitably watching him check the binding authority forms for another half-hour. What might be more interesting for me would be to go up to the third floor of the old Lloyd's across the road, and talk to Frank Barber, who had been the syndicate's underwriter for nearly thirty years and was a famous non-marine man.

Frank Barber turned out to be a large, expansive grey-haired man who is regarded with considerable affection in the market. He said he heard that I was writing something about Lloyd's, but seemed modestly surprised I'd come to see him. 'I thought it was going to be another of those books about marine underwriting,' he said, and roared with laughter.

I asked him about his syndicate, and he said that as the ex-underwriter it kept his name. As long as he was alive, it would remain Frank Barber and Others. When he died, if Malcolm was still the underwriter, it would take his name. The syndicate had 1,000 names or thereabouts, with a capacity of £30m, meaning that this was the maximum premium it was allowed to write by the Council.

Frank Barber himself is proud of having come up the hard way. He left school at sixteen, he said, had done two years at Lloyd's before volunteering for the RAF, and they had kept his job warm. After the war he had progressed to doing simple endorsements of policies and then renewals and straightforward new business. From there he went on to become an underwriter specializing in American business.

At this point we were joined by Jack Beecham, another former underwriter from the syndicate who told me he had written amusement parks and libel. I asked if the amusement parks weren't a fairly uncertain risk, and he said they certainly were. 'You can get some degree of inspection, and in the US they've got some codes of safety. But it's a very hazardous business.' The syndicate had had a couple of major losses in California when a lot of people fell off the big sky-wheel—it had cost the underwriters about $200,000, which had been a large sum in those days. The other thing was that it was often practically impossible to tell if someone was making a truthful claim or not. 'You get some people who'll pretend there was something faulty with the machinery. They've only got to step off a roundabout backwards and it's worth $200 to them.'

I asked if they included circuses with amusement parks and Jack Beecham looked cautious.

'Not since we had a circus where an elephant lifted its picket stake, which is the thing it's tied to when the circus isn't working. Well, this elephant wandered round the town, just for a walk, I suppose, and it came to an open lot where there was a truck parked. It started scratching its bottom on the side of the truck, and it was still doing it when the driver came back. I suppose he'd been drinking in some bar, and he didn't believe it when he saw the elephant. So he started belting it, and I'm afraid the elephant sat on him. That cost us $43,000.'

I wondered how the syndicate came to write these rather unusual risks, amusement parks and libels. Frank Barber explained that the syndicate had started in 1928, and the underwriter in those days had been a man with a typically Lloyd's feeling for innovation. The tradition had grown up that the syndicate was ready to look at any unusual class of business, and the tradition had stuck.

From the amusement parks we moved on to libel. Jack Beecham said that most provincial newspapers insure, but London ones don't—in the case of a mass circulation paper, the premium would be so big, it wouldn't be worth it. Once, one of the weeklies had had a policy with the syndicate, and there had very nearly been a big claim when a reviewer had written about a book by Lord Beaverbrook. The reviewer had implied that Beaverbrook tended to put a rather good complexion on his own part in recent history, and Beaverbrook had issued a writ.

The upshot had been that Jack Beecham had spent a whole day rushing round in taxis getting hold of solicitors, brokers and various editorial people. At last he had returned home, pretty well exhausted, and turned on the radio to hear the news that Lord Beaverbrook had died suddenly.

'It was,' he said, 'just about the most dramatic end to a libel case you could imagine.'

We came back to the syndicate itself. What did Frank Barber see as the real skill of underwriting? He said it was three things—attracting brokers to your box, not being afraid to write a big commitment on the good business and turning down the bad. 'When you look at it, unlimited liability's a marvellous principle,' he said. 'It's like what Dr Johnson said about the man being hanged. It concentrates the mind wonderfully.'

Because he himself came up the hard way, Frank Barber has strong feelings about helping the young staff on the box. It is a source of pride for him that the majority have come to Lloyd's without help from family connections. 'As soon as they demonstrate their commitment to the syndicate,' he says, 'we want to make them members.'

He has strong views about another idea now gaining ground at Lloyd's. His managing agency is a partnership which enables it to be easily handed on to others. Whereas in the past it has been the common practice to sell syndicates, often for very large sums, he believes Lloyd's long-term interests are best served by taking the partnership route. 'What is the point,' he asks, 'in making millions you can't spend and at the same time losing control of what you do best? The much better alternative is to pass it on to younger colleagues who have supported you loyally and enabled you to do well yourself.' His view, as I was to learn later on, is very much the spirit of the new Lloyd's.

5
The Brokers' Men

ONE of the astonishing things about the City of London is the number of large and prosperous firms you have never heard of. In ten minutes' walk around Leadenhall Street you will see so many merchant banks, investment companies and discount houses that you wonder how they all make a living.

Among those who make their bread and butter with jam are the insurance brokers. Around 260 of them are credited to Lloyd's, which entitles them to put 'and at Lloyd's' on their notepaper as if it was their country seat.

At the top of the pyramid are the seven known, with respectful envy, as the 'broker barons'. These are the firms of C. T. Bowring, Hogg Robinson, C. E. Heath, J. H. Minet, Alexander Howden, Sedgwick, and Willis, Faber and Dumas.

Today such firms are among the biggest invisible exporters in the City. Sedgwick, for example, goes back to the last century, when the names of Price, Forbes, Sedgwick and Collins were all famous in the market. Frank Collins, who joined up with Sedgwick in 1912, was a bearded patriarch noted in the City for the fact that he drove himself there every morning from the suburbs in a hansom. Meanwhile Price and Forbes had merged in 1893 to form Price, Forbes and in 1972 this firm merged with Sedgwick Collins. Brokers tend to get taken over or merge so often that you get an almost kaleidoscopic effect. Seven years later Sedgwick Forbes, as it then was, joined up with yet another broker, Bland Payne.

By now, as if the name-game had become too complicated, the firm became simply Sedgwick, and the vast firm it had become moved from its previously scattered offices to a new site west of Aldgate. But the new building was hardly in use before it became too small. Today the group—reckoned to be the world's second biggest broker—resides in the huge Sedgwick Centre in Aldgate where the visitor passing through the entrance hall may feast his eyes on John Piper's superb tapestries of the City gates—and learn the awesome statistic that, until the recent spread of telefax, there passed nightly through Sedgwick's telex room one per cent of the United Kingdom's entire telex traffic.

Nearly two-thirds of the risks placed by Lloyd's brokers are from the United States; all the main offices have links with companies in the major American cities, who are known variously as correspondents or producers. If a hotel group or an airline wants to insure, they will probably go direct to one of the big brokers in New York or Chicago. Small-town brokers will pass some risks to what are known as the surplus-line brokers, who deal in the kind of specialized insurance for which they will look to Lloyd's.

Thus the risks which arrive in the Room via the brokers' offices may have started anywhere from Seattle to Canyon City. 'In London,' said one Chicago broker, 'if you ask people the way to Lloyd's they're quite capable of directing you to the bank. At home you mention Lloyd's of London, and everyone's heard of it.'

At the heart of this reputation is Lloyd's willingness to take risks that no one else will look at. One broker told me that among the more precarious insurances he had placed was one for stock-car racing in Ohio. 'I was stopping in a small town when this guy came up and said he'd heard I was from Lloyd's. He promoted stock-car racing and wondered if I could get him some liability insurance to cover accidents to spectators. I shuddered. They'd got thousands of country people on a day out, and the only protection was a few barrels. Most of the cars were home-made and they had these bloody great engines, aero-engines mostly. I think we were crazy, but we placed it. We had claims all right—wheels disappearing into the crowd, felling little Freddy. All the same I don't think anyone got killed.'

What does an insurance broker actually do? Historically the verb 'to broke' has the same origin as 'to broach'. A broker, says the Oxford Dictionary, is 'one who acts as a middle-man in bargains'. At Lloyd's people talk about 'broking' somebody in the sense of selling them something.

If you want to insure your house or your car, you may quite possibly go to an insurance company direct. If the risk is a little more complicated or specialized, you will need to go to a broker. He will then shop around the various companies and try to get you the best terms, taking his own commission.

If on the other hand your risk is something like an oil rig or a petrochemical plant, then the chances are that you will need one of the brokers accredited to Lloyd's, whose representatives are the only people allowed to do business in the Room. Each day around 3,000 of their brokers circulate in it, and could be said to be its life-blood. Underwriters occasionally say hard things of brokers, but cannot do without them—if no brokers come to an underwriter's box, he does no business. Basically, the relationship remains good, if only because it has to. 'Broker and underwriter stay on good terms,' said one broker, 'because we both want to be in business tomorrow.'

In essence the code which governs dealing between the two is simple. If the underwriter asks the broker something that is not on the slip and he knows the answer, he is bound to give it. If the broker has information which could materially affect the risk but fails to give it, it is called a 'pick-up'. In practice this almost never happens, if only because a broker who did pick an underwriter up would soon get known in the market.

I asked one leading marine underwriter how often he had been picked up in his time at Lloyd's, and he said only once that he could swear to, but probably a few other times when he suspected it but couldn't prove it. 'I'd say there were three kinds of brokers in the Room,' he told me. 'There are those who wouldn't let me write a risk if they thought there was anything wrong with it. There are the great majority who are perfectly trustworthy, but you've got to read the slip. Finally, and very rarely, there are a few who'd deliberately try to mislead you.'

One senior broker told me that the proportion who occasionally picked up an underwriter was certainly less than five per cent. 'If you find you've got a pick-up artist on your staff,' he said, 'you have no choice but to remove him from the front line or remove him altogether. There's no question that standards here are higher than in any other market. Your personal integrity is the only thing you've got that's worth a row of beans.'

Brokers come in all shapes and sizes. There are experts who specialize in anything from oceanology to bloodstock. There are long-haired young brokers who get decanted from vans, a bit like police at a demonstration, at ten o'clock every morning outside the Room. There are cheerful middle-aged men in pinstripes who tend to call the underwriters 'Sir'. (Though this is not invariably a mark of respect. One broker told me he might call an underwriter 'sir' if he thought he wasn't being helpful.)

All insurance men have to be optimists but with the brokers it physically shows, a sort of enthusiastic glow like a comedian's smile for his entrance. 'The moment a broker goes into the Room,' said one, 'it's got to be the finest risk he's ever seen. Even when he's been turned down on some terrible risk the good broker will go round looking puzzled, wondering why the hell he couldn't place it. In the last analysis you broke yourself. That's the real secret.'

Even so, the 'hard' market that has prevailed since 1985—meaning that underwriters have been able to get higher rates—has meant tougher times for younger brokers. 'There are a lot of young brokers who've never known conditions as they are today,' I was told by one senior Willis Faber man. 'Some firms have even brought a few of their old war-horses out of retirement to help them.'

Built in almost as much as the broker's optimism is a sort of hectic energy. A lot of brokers give the impression of visibly burning themselves up, which may be worth it, when you consider that a six figure income is not unusual for a top broker. A director of one firm told me he'd be away on Thursday, he had to go to a two-hour meeting in Los Angeles and thought he might drop in to see a couple of people in New York on the way back, but hoped to be home by Sunday. I asked another broker what he did at weekends. 'Walk,' he said, making it sound like the training for a marathon of some sort. 'My wife and I walk along the beach at Bexhill. We're always walking. We must walk for bloody miles.'

Peter Wright, a former member of the Committee of Lloyd's, put the broking business in a nutshell. He had first come to the market in the mid-forties, and loved every minute of his time there. 'Once they let me into the market,' he reminisced, 'I knew that it was my world. I handled it my way. I realized it was all a matter of personal relationships, and it still is. How else do you persuade an underwriter to give you a reasonable rate on fresh eggs in paper bags from Montevideo to Liverpool?'

When it came to a big risk—say a North Sea construction platform—underwriters were going to have a lot of worries. 'Our job's to put their fears to bed. A broker's got to be a psychologist and a salesman put together.' Sometimes, he added, it could leave you physically drained and sometimes, when placing some enormous risk that would have to be shared out among several underwriters, he would go to one box and broke it to him for half an hour. 'Then I'd come away exhausted, so drained that I had to get out of the Room and go for a walk by the river before I tackled the next underwriter.'

How far, I asked him, would a broker actually go to get the best terms for a customer wanting insurance—was it a bit like a barrister trying to make out the best possible case for his client?

Peter Wright looked thoughtful, and replied that he didn't think it was quite the same. 'A barrister hopes not to see his client a second time. I want to go on doing business with mine and what's more important I've got to go on doing business with the underwriter.' There were brokers, he said, who would try to get the rates down so far that they practically ruined the market. 'When they drive too hard a bargain it doesn't help anyone. If things go wrong, they'll just have a tougher job to place the business next year.'

I asked him if he would always tell the underwriter all the facts about a risk and he said he would, except that like any salesman the broker's job was to put the facts in the best light. 'The bottle is always half full, never half empty. I don't have to put ideas into his head. If I'm placing a drilling-barge in the Gulf of Mexico, I wouldn't think it necessary to tell an underwriter that they get hurricanes there. Or, for that matter, that earthquakes happen in California or that the Baltic ices up. I don't have to tell him things he's deemed to know in the normal course of business.' All the same, he said, you could never forget that the relationship with the underwriter mattered: his loyalty was to Lloyd's as well as to his own firm.

Having said which, there were obviously different ways in which you might approach an underwriter, or which broker you might send to him. 'Suppose you have an underwriter who's a Rotarian. If you had an awkward risk to show him you might send a broker who was another Rotarian. Once we had a broker who was rather theatrical, a bit camp. We'd often send him with a difficult risk because he'd have them all rolling with laughter on the box and they'd write it.'

How competitive, I asked, was the world of the broker? A few days before, I had gone round with a young aviation broker who had suddenly dashed across the Room after another broker. The point was that he had seen him going to a box where he himself had already discussed a particular risk. We arrived just as the other broker was showing the underwriter the slip.

'I rather think we're on the same business.' The broker I was with looked mildly indignant, the underwriter looked mildly amused, the other broker looked mildly crestfallen.

'I don't think there's much I can do.' The underwriter gave the other man a tolerant nod. 'My rule is to favour the holding broker.' The other man went off, still looking crestfallen, and the broker I was with wished him better luck next time. He didn't seem ironic, simply friendly.

I told Peter Wright this story and he said this sort of thing went on in the market all the time. It was all part of trying to get the best terms for your client, and any broker in the market had to be constantly looking over his shoulder to see what the opposition were up to. Meanwhile, in the case of a very big risk, a client might ask several firms to produce a report. 'Over the next few years someone's going to want to insure the Channel Tunnel. They'll probably put the insurance out to tender among half a dozen brokers, who will put it together in various ways, with different rates, higher or lower deductibles and so on. Even so, the successful firm would probably be the one that had the best working relations with underwriters.'

The travels of brokers would make a theme for a modern Hakluyt. David Bridges, of Willis Faber and Dumas, often leaves his Cotswolds home on a Saturday morning for Heathrow, en route for the Middle East or Asia. Over lunch in the Captains' Room he mused over some other recent culinary treats; in the last two weeks, he said, he had drunk sour camel's milk with a sheikh and eaten sea-slugs in Beijing. Brokers nowadays, he explained, had to learn some curious things. In Thailand, for example, it was unwise to eat too much of the first course, however succulent, because it might be only the first of a possible fourteen. 'When you sit with a Thai, it's discourteous to sit with your feet towards him. In Arab countries when you're summoned to a feast of mutton, you must eat only with your right hand, because traditionally the Bedouin used to use his left for more fundamental matters.'

I asked how he had picked up so much exotic lore, and he explained that as a director of Willis's Oil and Gas Division he was placing reinsurances for national insurance companies in the Third World. 'In most Arab countries, for instance, the national oil company has to insure with a national insurance company, which in turn could need as much as ninety-five per cent reinsurance in the London and international markets.' Most insurers out there, he added, had fixed links with a London broker. As to the oil companies, their financial directors were usually members of the ruling family with whom he had become friends through helping them to plan their insurance programmes. On his last trip, a sheikh had insisted on his spending the afternoon showing Bridges his falconry. 'Those hawks lived in marble halls that you or I would be proud to live in.'

But travel in the Middle East is not all hawks and feasting. The oil companies work from 7 a.m. till 2 p.m., and the insurance companies work through the morning and then again in the afternoons from four till seven. 'Even apart from jetlag and the heat and humidity it can be punishing,' Bridges says. 'The difference is when you get to know the people. For the first few years it was always meals in the hotel. Nowadays I spend nearly all the time in the local Arabs' homes. It's the old Bedouin idea of hospitality. If you're passing through, then come and sit with me. I rather like that.'

Among the 6,000 brokers' men at Lloyd's there is nowadays an increasing number of women. They have followed the elegant example of Mrs Liliana Archibald, who became Lloyd's first woman broker in 1971 and later the London market's leading expert on EEC insurance. The last fifteen years has seen a female invasion which has not only made the Room a more decorative place but also made a decisive contribution to the market.

Does a girl broker get an easier ride from underwriters? The general view among the girls themselves is that while some might need to flirt with an underwriter to establish a rapport, just as some broking-house directors would send a pretty girl round to discuss a sticky claim, the majority seek to be taken on their merits. True, legend has it that the Superintendent of the Room once felt it necessary to send out a discreet directive suggesting that women should stop wearing too-tight tee-shirts. 'There are still,' says Jean Taylor, a director of Jardine, Thompson Graham, 'a few people in the Room for whom women brokers are a culture-shock. But, as a generalization, the way our business is conducted is changing, getting more graduate-oriented. You get more thinking people, less of the dining and wining type. I think most male graduates of my generation have grown up with the idea that women are their equals in the workplace.'

At thirty Jean Taylor herself is already highly-regarded in the aviation market. Meeting her, you sense a formidable skill and decisiveness behind her engaging, friendly manner. At Oxford, she told me, she had read Modern Languages; in 1978, when she came down, the university careers office had suggested she might go in for broking. 'They said linguists tend to be good brokers because they've got the gift of the gab,' she smiles. She had seen several firms and chosen Jardines. She had started broking in the Room almost at once. 'I didn't find it frightening. It was exciting,' she recalls. After two years she had decided to specialize in aviation reinsurance, partly because it interested her and also, she admits, 'because reinsurance is regarded as more glamorous outside the market. If you meet someone at a party and say that you're in insurance, they tend to equate it with selling encyclopaedias. Reinsurance has more style, like merchant banking.'

I asked her what the work actually involved, and she said that the point of excess-loss reinsurance, which she centres on, was to protect the direct insurer against what Lloyd's people casually call 'catastrophe'—the kind of disaster involving huge liability claims—which is particularly relevant in aviation. 'What happens is that an insurer—it may be a Lloyd's underwriter or a company specializing in aviation—asks us to arrange an excess-loss programme for him. He would tell me how much liability he wishes to assume, and I would then help him determine what size of line he should write and what income this will produce. The line might be $1m on the aircraft hull and $5m on passenger liability. So for the overall line of $6m, we then arrange excess-loss by means of a series of layers. Each of these would be rated separately, and led by different leading underwriters. By carefully thought-out layering, you can improve the overall cost. What I'm really doing in placing any reinsurance is the laying-off and spreading of the risk—using the market to the advantage of my client.'

There could hardly be two more different insurance institutions than Lloyd's and the People's Insurance Company of China. One is capitalist and three hundred years old. The other is state-owned and a relatively recent addition to the world's insurance markets.

Yet the rapport between the two is an important marker for the future, and to see why, it is perhaps necessary to look back at recent history for a moment. China, in pre-Mao Tse Tung days, had a well-developed insurance industry. Then came the Cultural Revolution, in which most skilled insurance men were forced to work at back-breaking field labour along with pianists and artists. Virtually the only policies to be written at all were those on marine cargoes, because it would have been impossible for the country's trade to move without them. When the Cultural Revolution came to an end in 1979, insurance was among the professional skills to surface after a long drought.

So the Chinese insurance industry had much to offer, and much to learn, for liberalization, when it eventually came, found an insurance industry whose practitioners were either older, or very young. Because of the rigours of the Cultural Revolution, insurance skills had simply skipped a generation.

Lloyd's response to the new situation of a re-emergent China came initially from the brokers, as I learnt from Sedgwick's China expert, David Brewer. In general terms, he told me, the PICC is even-handed in the way it passes on its major reinsurances to different world markets, and within those markets, to different brokers. Sedgwick's own main links with the PICC are on energy and nuclear risks. Willis Faber is similarly linked on marine, and Bowring on aviation. In 1985, when Lloyd's Chairman, Peter Miller, made a two-week tour of China, the brokers' role was acknowledged by the fact that, for the first time on a Chairman's foreign tour, he was accompanied by brokers—John Nightingale of Bowring, Michael Faber of Willis Faber, and David Brewer.

An earlier and vital link between the Chinese industry and London had come in 1979, when the then Sedgwick chairman, Neil Mills, was invited to Beijing to visit the head office of PICC, which was and still is, says David Brewer, 'the window for all the reinsurance coming out of China'. Brewer, who had already spent three years in Tokyo and spoke Japanese, was given the task of finding ways in which his company could best help the emergent PICC. Having broached the idea with PICC vice-chairman Lin Zheng-Feng, Sedgwick opened its own office in Beijing the following year. Initially run by Tim Mathieson and currently by Stephen Crabb—both brokers are products of Leeds University's Chinese School—the new office provided a focus for Sedgwick's business and a direct link into London for PICC. 'This is important,' says David Brewer, 'when other international markets are competing for their business.' Among the major risks it is currently handling is the reinsurance for China's first nuclear power station at Daya Bay—so vast a project that three Sedgwick technical experts have spent, to date, two-and-a-half years working on it.

Above all, what David Brewer finds fascinating and rewarding about the China link is the sense of mutual exchange after virtually thirty years of silence. 'What is exciting,' he says, 'is the opportunity of working with the bright young men and women who are the future leaders of the insurance business in China.' The benefits are mutual—Lloyd's, by sharing its experience, is able to contribute to the growth of PICC, and in turn attracts additional reinsurance business to London.

A lot of people at Lloyd's will insure you against the more predictable disasters. Only one set of people will insure you against the unlikely ones. These are the contingency brokers, and their world is original, unique, and highly expert. Most brokers pride themselves on being large but the contingency brokers take an esoteric pleasure in being small. There is only one firm of them, Adam Brothers Contingency Ltd, which I found in St Helen's Place, a pleasant and quietly elegant courtyard close to St Helen's Church, whose records include the name of William Shakespeare as a ratepayer of the parish.

To find out what goes on in the world of contingency broking, I talked to the chairman, Peter Nottage, a tall quiet man who looks like a senior diplomat, and two of his fellow directors, Geoff Fox and Harvey Hine, whose father had been largely instrumental in setting up the business.

How, I asked them, would they define contingency broking? Mr Hine said the best way would be to explain how the firm had developed its special interest. The original Adam Brothers were shipowners at Aberdeen. In 1882 they decided to become Lloyd's brokers in the marine market, mostly insuring their own ships. In the earlier part of this century the firm had found itself in the doldrums and started looking round for new men and new business. Harvey Hine's father had come in in 1936 and been followed a few months later by a man called Donovan Parsons, who had already worked at Lloyd's but had left and gone to Malaya to plant rubber. He had returned to London and to Lloyd's, but an important part of his interests and talent were in the theatre. 'It was really Parsons who triggered us off,' said Harvey Hine, 'because he had a talent as a lyric-writer which led to his getting to know a lot of theatre people in the West End. Parsons decided there was a form of insurance needed for when a theatrical star failed to appear, and the management lost money.'

Within a couple of years the new idea of insuring the non-appearance of stars was booming. Peter Nottage reeled off a list of people they had insured in the early days—Gordon Harker, Leslie Henson, Jack Hulbert and Cicely Courtneidge. Nowadays, he said, it was the equivalent of an international casting directory of the entertainment business.

As Europe drifted towards World War II, it began to occur to other people besides theatrical impresarios that anything from a trade fair to the Royal Tournament might not happen. They took out abandonment cover with the Lloyd's underwriters who had helped Adam Brothers to start the market. The firm, added Mr Hine, had gone on from there. Some of their business is handled direct, but most is passed on to them by other Lloyd's brokers who acknowledge their expertise. 'Really we provide a service to other brokers,' Geoff Fox put in. 'A lot of brokers tend to feel out of their depth when faced with an unusual risk. They know they can put an impossible proposition to us and we can handle it.'

Peter Nottage produced a list of more than sixty different classifications for modern contingency insurance. There was *Force Majeure* and Frustration, Royal Tours, Exhibitions, Expeditions and Twins. There was Erroneous Duplication, which Peter Nottage said was useful if you were offering a prize for lucky numbers and your printer went berserk and printed the winning number five hundred times over. The sort of people who would take out such an insurance were those who run big lotteries in the USA and oil companies who gave prizes for the sort of scratch-off tickets you were given at filling stations with your petrol.

One of the more ticklish areas handled by contingency insurance is the possible cancellation of such events as royal weddings or other events involving heads of state. Lloyd's does not permit the market to write an insurance on the life of, say, the President of the United States. But if a planned tour or celebration was prevented from taking place because of, for example, illness, then the manufacturers of souvenirs—such things as tee-shirts or commemorative mugs—would lose out on their investments and Lloyd's does permit them to insure against the possibility of cancellation arising from almost any cause. For such events as the World Cup and Olympic Games, Adam Brothers regularly place insurance for the organizers, as well as the sponsors who lavish huge sums on advertisement hoardings round the ground for matches that will be seen worldwide on television. On the Mexico World Cup in 1986, said Peter Nottage, they had placed about £40m.

The worlds of showbiz and television nowadays offer more esoteric insurance needs than the original one of non-appearance. If an advertiser has spent large sums on hiring a famous personality to do a commercial which they plan to use for months ahead, they may need to insure against not only his disability or death, but also the possibility of what the brokers sedately call 'moral turpitude', meaning that if the celebrity was involved in some scandal, their costly commercials might be useless. Possibly the most outlandish cover ever requested by a film-maker came as a result of the sequence at the end of Stanley

Kubrick's film *2001—A Space Odyssey*, when the hero goes into orbit round the planet Uranus sending out signals to anyone who lived there. Because they felt the climax would have been made pointless if the existence of other creatures in space had been discovered before the film was shown, the producers wanted £2m worth of insurance against the discovery of intelligent life on other planets before the premiere.

But what I mustn't run away with, said Peter Nottage rather firmly, was the idea that their business was mostly concerned with films and football. Nowadays by far the largest sector involved commercial and financial institutions like banks and large exporters for whom today's sophisticated policies include cover against political risks—for example, a bank guarantee being called in by the overseas buyer even though an exporter has not contravened his terms of contract. Another form of cover is against the occurrence of the *force majeure* risks he had mentioned. For example, if a bank lends a large sum to a company which is installing a major power plant, the company's ability to repay the debt will depend on how soon the plant is completed and starts to pay off. But if the building of the new plant were to be unduly delayed, the company might be unable to pay off its debt. To take care of this possibility, he will insure against the *force majeure* risk.

Peter Nottage went on browsing through his book which lists the various forms of contingency insurance. 'Here's another one,' he said. 'A lot of people insure against the death or disability of judges. Take a firm which is engaged in some complex litigation. Suppose the court action is almost finished, and then the judge trying the case has a heart attack. That case is going to go back to square one and everything the firm has spent on legal fees has almost all been lost.'

Archaeological finds, said Geoff Fox, was another area where they placed a lot of business. Ever since the discovery of the Mithras Temple near the Mansion House, people having new office blocks built in the City have become wary of the possibility that their excavation might turn up some important archaeological find. 'What happens then is that the Department of the Environment requires work on the site to be deferred while the archaeologists explore it. So the company insures against the extra expense caused by any extended delay in construction.'

I said that the trouble with contingency insurance was that it began to make you feel that nothing anywhere was secure. Peter Nottage laughed and said he supposed that was the nature of their business.

But he would give me a nice heartwarming little story to end with. It had concerned the explorer Wally Herbert, who had set out to cross the Arctic on foot in the 1960s. Herbert had been under contract to various newspapers to send them reports on his progress. Meanwhile his sponsors, the Royal Geographical Society, had taken the precaution of insuring against the expedition having to be abandoned. Indeed at one stage when he had to spend a winter in a hut near the Pole, things did look very bad for Herbert. 'What the underwriters did,' said Peter Nottage, 'was to make a sporting offer. They said they would charge a very high premium, around twenty per cent. If there was a claim they would keep the premium. If on the other hand Wally Herbert made it, they would return a big chunk of the premium. Herbert did make it, and on his return the Committee of Lloyd's gave him a lunch. At the end of the lunch they did something that Lloyd's never normally does. They gave him a cheque for a no-claims bonus.'

The clock in the dining-room at the Bowring Building has ticked away for nearly two centuries by now. It was made by Benjamin Bowring, who founded the firm in 1811. Both firm and clock are still in good shape.

Benjamin himself began as a clockmaker at Exeter, then went to Newfoundland, where he moved into shipping. By the 1820s he had his own wharf at St John's, besides two schooners and a brig used for whaling and the seal trade. The next generation of Bowrings saw the fleet expanding. Bowring ships would take dried cod from Newfoundland to Cadiz, then load wine for Liverpool, where they would pick up a cargo of the Cheshire salt needed for the fish-drying sheds at St John's. Over the next eighty years the family came to own sixty-two ships—among them the *Terra Nova*, which became the most famous of all Bowring ships when the firm lent her to Captain Scott for his last expedition. Moving into insurance from shipping was a natural step, George Bowring, grandson of Benjamin, began broking marine policies at Lloyd's in the 1870s.

Since then, Bowring has become one of the great broking names of Lloyd's, and the modern company has one aspect which Benjamin would have been proud of: its American connection.

Ever since the turn of the century, American business has been closely linked to Lloyd's, whose underwriters insured everything from the San Francisco earthquake to saloons in downtown Chicago and the jewellery of Manhattan millionaires' wives. But, since Lloyd's may only accept risks from brokers accredited to the market, this huge flow of business has come in two separate stages. Stemming in the first place from American brokers, it has been actually placed in the market by their counterparts in London. Over the years, powerful links were thus set up between London and US brokers, known as their 'correspondents'.

One of the strongest was that between Bowring and the great broking house of Marsh & McLennan in New York. Indeed the link went back even earlier than the formation of Marsh & McLennan itself, to a famous American reinsurance man named Guy Carpenter, whose own firm they had taken over. It is part of American insurance folklore that Mr Marsh and Mr McLennan, having failed to persuade Guy Carpenter to sell them his business, learnt that he was sailing on a Cunarder from New York to London. With characteristic enterprise they bought themselves tickets for the voyage, and clinched the deal by the time the ship reached London.

Perhaps it was the same get-up-and-go spirit that, in the 1970s, caused Marsh & McLennan, by now the biggest insurance brokers in the world, to look for firmer footholds in the London market. For a new feeling had begun to surface among the mighty brokers of Manhattan. When they provided Lloyd's with so much of its business, the leading brokers felt, was it fair that they should continue to be treated as outsiders? Perhaps the feeling was not precisely put into words, but it was the essence of the new mood. By the mid-1970s Marsh & McLennan themselves had begun to discuss a possible merger or takeover of Bowring.

Part of their strategy at the time was to establish a global network. 'Already they had a strong minority participation in several leading European brokers,' says Bowring's chairman, Gil Cooke. 'Now they wanted to close ranks with their London brokers.' Thus the Committee of Lloyd's were faced with a dilemma. To allow the American brokers in would mean departing from tradition. To keep them out, on the other hand, would seem like biting, or at least insulting, the hand that fed them. Eventually Lloyd's accepted what seemed to be the spirit of the times. In April 1980, they agreed that Bowring could continue to be Lloyd's brokers if they became part of the Marsh & McLennan empire, provided there was no interference from the parent company with Bowring's activities at Lloyd's. In the event, no damage was done to either Lloyd's or Bowring's independence or tradition. 'Bowring, functioning as a wholly-owned subsidiary of Marsh &

McLennan, continues to conduct its Lloyd's business as it always has done. We're still a very British company,' says Gil Cooke.

Bowring is no longer a family firm in the sense that members of the family sit on the board. It does, however, have the sense of loyalty and continuity which comes of long tradition. Of the 3,500 people who work for it, 200 have over twenty–five years' service. Its specialities range from aviation—Bowring is the largest airline broker—to smaller-scale domestic business, in which it is the United Kingdom's largest retail broker. But by far the largest proportion of its business comes from the US, via the Marsh & McLennan connection. In the Lloyd's market, Bowring is by far the largest producer of American reinsurance business.

Almost as much as insurance itself, people at Lloyd's talk about reinsurance, the highly specialized and esoteric means by which underwriters offload part of their risk. Most reinsurances, I had learnt, are structured in huge and complex layers—and even then, the reinsurer will again lay off his liability in what is called a retrocession. I learnt something of their intriguing trade from Ivor Binney and Philip Wroughton, Bowring's two deputy chairmen, who are top experts in this side of the market. What kind of reinsurance risks, I asked, came from the US?

Philip Wroughton said most of the people they were reinsuring would be American insurance companies, who were themselves seeking to lay off their liabilities on anything from industrial risks like those of the Fortune 500 companies, to the chances of a San Francisco earthquake, which he thought spelt the largest potential danger to the London market.

How, I asked, did an earthquake risk compare with those like pollution and asbestosis, on which Lloyd's had recently paid out huge sums to industrialists who suddenly found themselves liable for compensation to their workforce?

Ivor Binney said the two things were difficult to compare. 'Asbestosis and pollution grow over the years. Each year the underwriter or the insurance company find they haven't reserved enough to pay for the claims, so they reserve a bit more. The difference with an earthquake or a major storm is that it comes at you all of a sudden. As opposed to a pollution claim which comes from way back in the past.'

Philip Wroughton nodded. 'We haven't had a San Francisco earthquake for eighty years and we don't know.' The other comparable threat, he said, was what insurance men call windstorm damage. In 1985, Hurricane Gloria had swept up the American east coast and then stopped offshore off Long Island. 'If it had hit Manhattan and Long Island, the companies who had it could have had liabilities up to seven billion dollars.'

'Could the Lloyd's market pay for another San Francisco earthquake?'

Ivor Binney looked up shrewdly. 'This market is based on the unlimited liability of its members. That means it will pay up. But there'd be a lot of insurance markets that could not pay.'

At the same time, he said, one mustn't think the underwriters weren't watching these things. 'They're logged very carefully by the syndicates that specialize in this type of business. Then they buy more reinsurance against their liabilities. It's not a haphazard game. It's a very carefully calculated business.'

I thanked the two of them and left. As I passed the dining-room, Benjamin Bowring's clock said half past five. In the cool air of a London evening, San Francisco and seven-billion dollar windstorms seemed a long way off.

I wondered if they seemed quite so remote to the cool men of Lloyd's, as they sat working out the bill they may one day be handed for another San Francisco earthquake.

A doorkeeper at
Lloyd's in 1890

Doorkeeper Peter Costen outside the New
Lloyd's

"A Glance at the
Loss Book"—from
the Illustrated London
News in 1890

Walter Farrant, Lloyd's most famous caller

The New Lloyd's seen from the fourth floor

The Underwriting Room at the Royal Exchange in 1900

6

Keeping the Coffee House

'SEDGWICK, Pennington, Hogg Robinson, Thompson.'

What we are listening to is perhaps the most characteristic of all sounds at Lloyd's. It is the perpetual background noise of the Room, the sound of brokers' names being intoned by the Caller from the Rostrum below the Lutine Bell. From nine-thirty in the morning till five in the afternoon it goes on. According to the Caller's intonation it can variably sound like electronic music, mediaeval plainsong or a muezzin's call to prayer.

'Willis Faber, Burroughs-Johnson.' A double-barrelled name seems to give the Caller more of an intonation to bite on: his voice goes up on the first and then down on the second syllable. John*song*—it sounds like a superior brand of tea. The tone is rhythmic, sonorous, and unique. In his red robe and velvet collar, the Caller is the direct descendant of the Kidney. But like many things at Lloyd's, calling is not done merely because it is time-honoured, but because it works.

The 260 broking firms attached to Lloyd's represent between them a total of around 5,000 brokers, any or all of whom could be milling about the Room at a given moment. Suppose an underwriter or someone else from their office wants to get hold of them? All he does is go to the Caller's rostrum and give the name of the man he wants. The Caller will then intone the names of the broking firm and the broker. The extraordinary thing is that the broker will hear it, even above the hum and babel of what is seldom less than three thousand people.

How, you may ask, does it work? Lloyd's explanation is simple. Because the noise is going on all the time, they say, you never hear the Caller's voice at all unless it is your own name he is calling. The explanation may sound unlikely, but one broker told me he could spend all day in the Room and never be aware of the Caller. 'Then at half-past four in the afternoon he calls your own name and it's as if someone had bawled it in your ear.'

The present doyen of the Caller's craft is Michael Crowley, who told me that he belongs to an operatic society at home in Harlow. He wasn't sure, he said, if it related very much—but calling became boring to the listener if you didn't do a bit of singing. 'A broker gets used to his own call and nothing else. I try to develop a style for each name.' If someone had a rather overworked name like my own name, Brown, he said they would usually agree on a pseudonym, his middle name for instance.

Learning to be a Caller takes about six months. Apart from developing the singing voice, he must become familiar with the names of all the broking houses. Mike Crowley himself calls for about two hours each day, the rest of the time being shared, in half-hour shifts, between six other members of the liveried staff who have qualified as callers. In the new Room, the actual calling is augmented by small video screens on which names are displayed for about thirty seconds after they have been called. While the Caller himself will announce only the broker's name and company, the screen will also inform him that he should, for instance, go to a particular box or call his office.

Historically, the list of Callers includes the name of one particularly famous Lloyd's man: Walter Farrant, who before he came to the market, worked on Windsor railway station as a porter. One day a Lloyd's underwriter noticed his sonorous style of calling the names of stations on the line from Windsor to Waterloo. The result was that Farrant became a legend as Lloyd's most famous Caller—and such a market institution that on his retirement *The Times* recorded the event with half a column.

In his traditional dress and position on the rostrum, the Caller is in a sense the archetypal figure of the coffee house, spanning three hundred years of history. Meanwhile Mike Crowley and his red-robed colleagues are no longer the only servants of Lloyd's. It is time now to move out from the Room and look at the Corporation.

The present Chief Executive of Lloyd's is Mr Alan Lord, and in the 1958 building, close to his office, there used to be a board on which you could see inscribed the names of all his predecessors. Strictly speaking, they were not his predecessors as Chief Executive for the title is a very new one. But in a broader sense Mr Lord is the modern version of the Master of the coffee house. The first name on the board is that of Edward Lloyd himself.

Following him there come the successive Masters down to 1804, in which year the office of Master of the coffee house lapsed. (Possibly it might have survived to this day had it not been for the snobbishness of a certain First Lord of the Admiralty who resented having to correspond on shipping intelligence matters with a person he called 'a waiter'. The members of Lloyd's, with a characteristically adroit touch, replied by merely promoting the Master to the post of Secretary, in which capacity the First Lord happily continued to correspond with him.)

Thus from 1804 onwards the chief administrator of Lloyd's was known as the Secretary. Perhaps the most distinguished of the Secretaries was Colonel Hozier, who came to Lloyd's in 1872, the year after it had been made a Corporation by Act of Parliament. In his reign the staff became greatly expanded and more efficient. It was Hozier himself who was largely responsible for the spread of Lloyd's signal stations and the creation of its world-wide system of overseas agents. Later he was knighted, and indirectly added to his distinctions by becoming the father-in-law of Sir Winston Churchill.

But the reason for singling out Hozier is not so much his service to Lloyd's as the insight we can get by comparing the Corporation of today with his time. Some of his office notebooks have been preserved, and a fascinating contrast they show us. When Hozier came to Lloyd's in 1872 the staff consisted of forty-four people, most of them engaged in the sort of work done by club servants. One page of his notebooks deals with what were called 'Servants' Allowances'. In it we read, for example, that the boys cleaning inkwells would get an extra 4s a week. For delivering Lloyd's Intelligence to newspapers after 5.00 p.m., they would get an extra 8s 6d a week, with a special fee of 4s a night for Christmas, Boxing Day and Easter Monday. Cleaning the members' lavatories rated 6s a week. The boy 'arranging policies', surprisingly, got only half-a-crown.

These allowances were in addition to the servants' ordinary weekly wages, which were hardly generous. Even as late as 1920 the *Daily Chronicle* carried small advertisements for 'respectable boys as messengers at Lloyd's. Wages 14s a week, uniform and boots supplied.'

Hozier himself, it is hard not to suspect, regarded it as a major objective to keep the wage-bill down. 'Wild will be retained on the establishment at the present rate of 17s 6d per week', runs a characteristically stern entry in the office notebook, 'but he must not expect any increase. Farrant's application for an increase of wage cannot be granted.' (This was the famous Walter Farrant, the Caller.) In 1880, we find Hozier instructing that 'in future boys shall leave the service of the Committee at 16 years of age instead of at 18 as at present'—the point being, presumably, that after 16, they would demand higher wages.

But what we do not get from Hozier's notebooks is any feeling that the Corporation staff were making a contribution to the real work being done at Lloyd's. The change over a hundred years is not simply that in his time there were forty-four people on the payroll and that there are now two thousand. The point is that nowadays the whole quality of their contribution is different.

Why, you might ask, if Lloyd's is so essentially based on individualism, does it need an organization at all? The point is that it is precisely because of the organization that the underwriter can remain an individual.

What it does, in effect, is to leave him free to get on with his underwriting.

The most obvious example of this is the department which controls the audit, not only monitoring the underwriters' assets but, from the public's point of view, ensuring the security of a Lloyd's policy. Yet the actual mode of the control works in such a way as to keep the bookwork, from the underwriters' point of view, to a minimum.

In an earlier chapter we saw how the underwriter, having completed his year's dealings, sends his books to be audited by an accountant approved by Lloyd's. Once the accountant has confirmed his figures, the auditor's report and certificate will go to the department for detailed checking.* Its role is an immensely responsible one, for it must keep a watchful eye on a constant stream of money, and at the same time be ready to detect any weakness in an underwriter's position. It must also see that the Department of Trade and Industry gets an Audit Certificate in respect of every underwriting syndicate. This shows that the underwriter has got sufficient assets to meet his losses.

But how is it possible to tell what his future losses may be? This will have been assessed by the auditors, according to a minimum standard based on past experience and what the underwriter himself thinks he needs to meet outstanding claims. In most cases the procedure is automatic and the underwriter's own estimate is accepted, though there may be half a dozen cases a year where the underwriting agent and the auditor don't agree. If this happens it is the job of the Audit sub-committee to sort it out.

Apart from the annual harvest of Audit Certificates, the Department is also responsible for much of the mountain of paper work which in a more conventional organization would clutter the underwriter's own desk. The Bank of England needs details of all the names' dollar hold-ings—these go direct from the Audit Office. If a name dies, there will be the question of withdrawing his deposit.

What about the other departments of the Corporation? If you look at a list of them you will find sixteen main ones ranging from Claims to Intelligence and Aviation. Among the most recently developed on a large scale is the Information Department. In its nature Lloyd's has always mirrored world events, and nowadays with such things as hijacking and pollution stories, Lloyd's increasingly makes news.

Though Lloyd's does not advertise, one aspect of the Information Department's work is to see that journalists are informed about the often subtle intricacies of underwriting business. Pamphlets and bro-chures are produced in more than a dozen languages. Upwards of 200,000 people are annually shown round Lloyd's—among them par-ties of provincial newspaper editors, foreign journalists and school careers masters who may be expected to introduce the underwriters of the future.

In terms of power the most important department is the Financial Comptroller's, which looks after Lloyd's various trust funds. Not all these are necessarily British-based. Sometimes an overseas govern-ment will insist that the resources to pay claims must be lodged in their own country, and if so it will be the responsibility of the Financial Comptroller's Department in London. So, too, is the money which Lloyd's invests from its various funds and deposits. 'Compared with a conventional insurance company,' I was told, 'it isn't all that much. Even so, an overnight fund of a few million pounds or so—a small merchant bank would quite like to have the handling of this sort of money.'

Although the Corporation is there primarily as a service to the underwriters, it also has the job of protecting the public and seeing that Lloyd's rules are observed. In the role of watch-dog is the Advisory and Legislation Department. Its job is to check on those risks which underwriters are not allowed to write. We saw, earlier for instance, how credit insurance—meaning the guaranteeing of someone's finan-cial stability—was banned after the Harrison case. War risks on land are also banned by agreement between all British insurers, because the amounts involved could be so astronomical that there would be no guarantee of all claims being met.

Increasingly there is also the problem of foreign legislation—although Lloyd's writes some form of insurance for almost every country in the world there are some whose national laws impose restrictions. In France, for instance, a foreign insurer can write non-marine but not marine business. Italy has a law which specifically prohibits insurance being placed with an individual as opposed to a company, which automatically excludes Lloyd's.

In recent years many of the developing nations have set up national insurance companies of their own with a prohibition on others. When this happens, Lloyd's reacts to the situation with a characteristic mixture of expertise and charm.

'If a country decides it's going to set up a company of its own,' one underwriter told me, 'we usually ask if they'd like any help. Quite often we'd send somebody out for a year or so to advise them on how to set up their office. There wouldn't be any strings attached, but in years to come it'd probably pay off in terms of making contacts.'

The Advisory Department also checks on some of the specific types of insurance which underwriters, for what one could call generally public-spirited and ethical reasons, are not allowed to write. Nobody can be insured at Lloyd's against the consequences of their own criminal actions—in other words if you were a burglar you wouldn't be able to get Lloyd's to insure you against breaking your leg in the line of duty.

Where anything can be even remotely held to be against the public interest, Lloyd's will not permit insurance. For instance it stays clear of disputes between capital and labour—an employer can't take up an insurance against his men going on strike, but equally a union itself cannot insure its members against loss of earnings during a strike.

The life of a head of state may not be insured, in case someone got to know what was the going rate at Lloyd's on their chances of assassination. You can insure against a General Election happening on a particular day to spoil your daughter's eighteenth birthday party, but not against the chance that the Tories or Labour might win. Political parties have been unable to insure since 1952, when Sir Eustace Pulbrook, a former Chairman of Lloyd's wrote a policy indemnifying Liberals against the loss of electoral deposits. What disturbed the Committee of Lloyd's was not so much that underwriters had had to pay upon a trail of Liberal lost deposits. It was that they might have seemed to be encouraging a certain frivolity among candidates.

Meanwhile how are the rules enforced? The most important and effective checkpoint is Lloyd's Policy Signing Office, which, working in conjunction with Lloyd's data-processing centre at Chatham, records the details of every policy issued. Since 1924 no policy has been recognized as valid unless it bears the official seal of the Signing Office. As they arrive from the brokers, all policies are checked by skilled examiners who will make sure there is no transgression of Lloyd's rules.

Once the policy is approved it goes to the Signing Section where it gets an official seal. Meanwhile all details of the risk are recorded on the Premium Advice Card produced by the computer; a copy of this will eventually go to both broker and underwriter.

The computers may seem a little out of place in the organization of the coffee house. In another sense they are the link between three hundred years of history and the future. They are the means by which Lloyd's individualism survives in the world of modern business communications.

'The management of this house has ever been the pride of my heart,' said one eighteenth century Master of the coffee-house, Thomas Taylor. For some of his recent successors, the job has been more like a nightmare. In the early 1980s the market was hit by a series of largely self-inflicted wounds which together make up Lloyd's darkest period since Angerstein drummed out the gambling underwriters in 1773.

What were the conditions that made it all but impossible in some months of 1982, to open the city page of any British newspaper without reading about some new scandal in the underwriting market? Perhaps the first thing we need to explore is the subtle relationship that had traditionally existed between the market and, as it was then, the Committee.

The Committee had always run the market on a loose rein, and until 1977 its weekly meetings in the eighteenth century panelled hall brought from Bowood House in Wiltshire—complete with chandeliers and Adam fireplace and now transported lock stock and barrel across Lime Street to the new Lloyd's—had been relatively untroubled. When it seemed necessary it had reacted to problems and threatening situations by the introduction of such measures as the Audit. But in general it had always been reluctant to impose what might seem to be bureaucratic rules. Perhaps a more significant nuance was the sense in which Lloyd's remained a club, whose members were sensitive about laying down the law to people who were friends and colleagues. Indeed, until very recently there was very little law to be laid down. The Committee of Lloyd's could not discipline anyone unless they were in clear breach of market regulations, while to expel a member required a special meeting of all members and a seventy-five per cent majority in favour of expulsion. 'In general,' said one Committee member, 'anyone who misbehaved outrageously was expected to resign. The Chairman would send for him and hand him a letter of resignation. The chap would sometimes huff and puff but he would always sign it.'

This was the situation in the late 1970s when the market suddenly began to buzz with disturbing rumours. They concerned an underwriter named Tim Sasse, who had been writing American fire insurance. Many of his risks were on ghetto properties in the South Bronx quarter of New York City. If you drive through that area today, you may still see burnt-down and looted houses in a scene of dereliction reminiscent of an air-raid. Sasse had written these policies on the binding authority principle by which a Lloyd's underwriter will assume risks that an appointed agent, who may function from anywhere in the world, has written for him. Underwriters, as we have seen, will usually only write a proportion of a risk. Sasse chose to write a hundred per cent of the business fed him by the brokers.

Up to this point Sasse had broken none of Lloyd's rules. He had fallen victim to, as one underwriter put it, 'people who were out to make a fast buck from the commission that arose from that great block of unplaceable business. These people always believe there's an idiot underwriter somewhere who can be found to write it.'

Things soon began going very badly wrong for Sasse, who had failed to appreciate that the business was taking him far beyond his premium limits. Looking back, it may be said they were going wrong for Lloyd's as well. There are many people in the market today who feel that the situation might have been saved or at least modified if the Committee had noticed the alarm bells sooner. In the absence of the firm action there might have been, the loss to the Sasse syndicate was £15m for 1976 and another £7m for the next year. In the event, Lloyd's bailed out the Sasse names to the tune of £16m. Nevertheless, there were names on the syndicates who lost their proverbial shirts. It was the first time in most peoples' memory that a large-scale underwriting loss had become a reality instead of a subject for gallows humour.

Meanwhile the Committee of Lloyd's, chaired by Ian Findlay, had already decided that it must take steps to put its house in order. To this end it had asked a working party, led by a former High Court judge, Sir Henry Fisher, to conduct a thoroughgoing review of the market and the rules under which it was run.

The Sasse affair had shown Lloyd's need to concern itself with the protection of its members—a need that was to be confirmed even more ominously later. The Fisher Committee, apart from Sir Henry himself, consisted of four Lloyd's men and two from outside. Appointments to it had been made in January 1979. One of the Lloyd's members, marine underwriter Gordon Hutton, told me he had been elected chairman of the Marine Underwriters Association one day in early January. When the Chairman of Lloyd's had sent for him on the same morning, he supposed it was to congratulate him on his new appointment. Instead he found himself drafted to what was to turn out to be an extremely onerous duty over two years. The Fisher Committee met altogether ninety times, hearing evidence from numerous market groups and often discussing the problems late into the evenings.

The Fisher Committee's fundamental aim was to bring Lloyd's into a new age, and it is perhaps worth stressing that Fisher did not tell Lloyd's anything it did not wish to hear. What the Committee sought, in effect, was an outside corroboration of its own awareness of the limitations of its powers. The methods that had worked very well in the 1871 and 1911 Lloyd's Acts needed adapting to the changing climate of the 1980s, and if there was to be a new Lloyd's Act it would need to take notice of the changes. 'What the Committee lacked was the ability to use disciplinary powers quickly and effectively,' says Gordon Hutton. 'There was a realization throughout the market that times had changed. The days had long since gone when a word from the Chairman was totally effective.'

Human vanity, folly and cupidity are not worth dwelling on unless one looks at the reasons why they happen. Behind the Lloyd's scandals of the 1970s and early 1980s one may trace a consistent pattern. Most of the later scandals were concerned with offshore funds, and those involved with them came from the generation which had come to Lloyd's in the immediate post-war years.

Those years were the first in which Britain became the most highly-taxed nation in Europe. Taxation had become identified with bureaucracy, and in some quarters it became seen as a legitimate skill—indeed almost as a virtue—to find some means to outwit the taxman. Soon there was hardly a respectable City company that did not have an accommodation address in some tax-free haven, varying in delectability from Bermuda to the Isle of Man, and these became natural homes for reinsurance funds garnered by less than scrupulous insurers.

There was another peculiarity in the Lloyd's system which had a bearing on the scandals. The later affairs of Howden and Cameron-Webb were to concern a broker involved with a syndicate, and *vice versa*. To see how this could happen, we need to look briefly at the relationship of syndicates and brokers.

Traditionally, until the end of the Second World War, most syndicates had been privately owned. But, from the late 1940s onwards, many syndicates had been sold to brokers. Once a price had been put on one successful syndicate, it was often hard for others to resist the temptation of a high price. Later the broker–syndicate link came to be perceived by many outside Lloyd's—particularly in Parliament—as unethical. A broker, it was said, would be bound to exert influence on his own syndicate to persuade the underwriter to accept bad business. In practice, most Lloyd's men will tell you, this never happened. But there are many people in the market who will also tell you that it was a bad day for Lloyd's when the syndicates were put on sale.

What one can see, looking back, is that the broker–syndicate links were an enormous help to many ambitious young men who, in the later 1940s, were looking for a means of acquiring money tax-free. For a young man back from the war with no Lloyd's family connections, the natural route would be to find a backer among the broking houses. The broker would agree to provide him with an office and an underwriting set-up. Before long he might expect to have his own syndicate alongside the one where he was writing for the broker, and he would soon find himself sitting on a source of tax-free wealth. Thus the selling of the syndicates had opened up the way to the pot of gold—the opportunity for tax-free profits. Arguably, it may also have helped to create the climate in which the 1982 frauds took place. Certainly those involved were all of the generation that had profited by them.

Some of these aspects may have been in the back of the Fisher Committee's minds when they sat down in 1979 to examine Lloyd's, but they were not their prime consideration. This was to consider the whole question of self-regulation in the market, bearing in mind the Committee's own desire for powers which might help to prevent a recurrence of a disaster on the scale of Sasse. For the next two years the Fisher Committee deliberated, and on 27 June 1980 their report was published. Its main conclusion was that a new Act of Parliament would be needed to strengthen Lloyd's own powers of self-regulation. The Committee, they thought, should be replaced with a larger body called the Council. This would consist of sixteen working members, six more drawn from the names, or non-working members, and three unconnected with Lloyd's, who would be nominated by the Governor of the Bank of England. Additionally, Fisher proposed, the practice of brokers owning syndicates should be discontinued. There were to be new and more stringent rules on the use of the binding authorities which had led to Sasse's downfall. The measures towards tighter control were along lines that the Committee itself had long sought. There would be no more easygoing management of the market. 'The elite club of Lime Street will never be quite the same again,' *The Times* said in a leader.

The members of the Committee actually received their copies of the Fisher Report in a setting reminiscent of diplomats being handed peace-plans; for a whole weekend they were immured in a large suite at the Hilton. The members having read and digested each section, it was then debated before they went on to the next bit. 'We had too much to do even to go out for a walk,' recalls Frank Barber. 'When you weren't working you were eating and when you were eating you were working as well. From it all, there sprang the tremendous changes we imposed on ourselves.' Another Committee member, Ivor Binney, found that the Sunday morning of the Hilton weekend clashed with his daughter's confirmation. He was allowed out for a couple of hours to attend it, then returned like a parole prisoner to the Hilton.

In the event the whole of the Fisher Report was embodied in the new Lloyd's Act which became law on 23 July 1982. All in all, it was agreed that the Act would give the new Council the required new powers of regulation. Meanwhile, through most of 1982, Lloyd's had continued to be in the news. During the passage of the Bill through Parliament, there had been considerable debate over the question of whether there should be what Fisher had called 'divestment', or separation of the syndicates from the brokers, and this had eventually been included. Intrigued City editors had also lavished many column-inches on the rearguard action of the Sasse names to obtain what they saw as reasonable redress from Lloyd's against their losses.

Otherwise, the Committee—shortly due to become transformed

into the Council—might have reasonably hoped that the talk of scandals would slowly die down. But on 22 September, barely a month after the Royal Assent to the Lloyd's Act, there came the first hint of an affair that was to take Lloyd's into still murkier waters.

The new problem concerned an old-established broking house named Alexander Howden. A year previously, following the same path as Bowring's relationship with Marsh & McLennan, Howden had been taken over by another giant American broker named Alexander and Alexander.

It had not been till after the takeover that Alexanders found some odd discrepancies in the Howden books. Several million pounds appeared to have gone missing, and the market rumour was that they had been channelled through what was described as 'a cosy reinsurance arrangement' with companies controlled by former Howden officials.' Among the names mentioned was that of Kenneth Grob, the former Howden chairman. On 21 September *The Times* reported that the Department of Trade had ordered a full investigation into the affairs of the Alexander Howden Group, as a result of an 'explosive document' filed with the United States Securities and Exchange Commission by Alexander and Alexander Services, alleging misappropriation of funds on a massive scale. 'The City of London Fraud Squad,' the report added ominously, 'will be investigating.'

Lloyd's had become news, and now not only on the financial pages. For many weeks that autumn Sunday newspaper readers were regaled with details of Grob and his friends' exotic life-style. The reinsurance funds, it seemed, had been converted into such handy possessions as a controlling share in a Swiss bank, Grob's own multi-million pound villa near Cap Ferrat, and several Impressionist paintings. The Committee, now only weeks away from the new regime that they had hoped was going to resolve Lloyd's problems, could do nothing but read and shudder.

Nevertheless, they put the best face they could upon things. On 12 October Lloyd's then Chairman, Sir Peter Green, was quoted in a stoutly defensive interview in *The Times*. 'We have been given,' he told the interviewer, 'an Act of Parliament under which we will be given great powers to devise a new method of self-regulation.' Ten days later, Sir Peter admitted in a speech at the annual Bankers' Dinner at Guildhall that the market was 'once again in the throes of scandal'. Had he but known, the scandals so far were as nothing compared with what was to follow.

The first mention of the PCW affair came on 2 November, when Lloyd's Information Department gave out a terse announcement. It stated that Peter Dixon, chairman of the PCW agencies (PCW stood for Peter Cameron-Webb, the underwriter) had voluntarily suspended himself from his duties.

What lay behind this statement was that the Committee had learnt that Cameron-Webb had, like the Howden four, been siphoning reinsurances to companies in which he had an interest. It was the old story of tax-free funds offshore, but this time with a new twist: the people Cameron-Webb had been defrauding were his own names. It seemed that what he had perfected was a Lloyd's version of what the Stock Exchange calls insider dealing. In the first place he had set up his own offshore company to cut his reinsurance costs. Then he had gone on to place the relatively safe risks with his own company. If there were no claims, the premium which his names had paid would go into his pocket. In the end he had gone on to placing large amounts of his syndicate's reinsurances with his own companies, with no intention of accounting for them.

Lloyd's had always optimistically maintained that occasionally you got a rotten apple in a barrel, but it seemed the rottenness was spreading. By the end of November it had become clear that Minets, the brokers who sponsored Cameron-Webb, were implicated, and the resignation of their chairman, John Wallrock, followed his admission that he had also profited from the Cameron-Webb frauds. On 30 November, Lord Cockfield, the Secretary of State for Trade, met Sir Peter Green to discuss Lloyd's self-regulation under the new Act which would be in force in one month. 'With this new framework in place,' ran Cockfield's statement, 'there will be a general expectation of prompt action by the Lloyd's authorities as particular issues arise.' Because of the Cameron-Webb affair, the Government was able to insist on a draconian step which Lloyd's had till then resisted. This was the appointment of an outside Chief Executive as a nominated member of the Council. He would rank as Deputy Chairman, and would be answerable to the Governor of the Bank of England for the proper running of the market.

Although Lloyd's has exercised its own disciplinary powers, none of the people who brought Lloyd's into disrepute have yet been prosecuted. The Howden affair is as yet unresolved. John Wallrock, the ex-Minet chairman, lives in exile in Hong Kong, and Tim Sasse is dead. Both Cameron-Webb and Peter Dixon have so far chosen to stay

away from Britain. Dixon has been fined £1m by Lloyd's, who have yet
to see the colour of his money. After living for some time in Marbella,
he skipped to the USA when Britain renewed its extradition treaty with
Spain. Cameron-Webb, at the time of writing, is still sunning himself
on, as the *Economist* put it, 'one of his (or more correctly his ex-names')
yachts in the Caribbean'.

As to Lloyd's itself, a new phase in its history began on 5 January
1983 with the first full meeting of the new Council. For a while, in the
wake of the Cameron-Webb affair, there were rumours of new frauds,
as if the contagion might be never-ending. But gradually they died
down and—though sadly for himself and Lloyd's, Sir Peter Green was
later fined and censured for negligence in relation to his names'
funds—new scandals failed to surface.

Nevertheless, Lloyd's more outspoken critics continued to demand
that the market should be placed under some form of external supervision—an issue which was eventually resolved in January 1987 when
the committee headed by Sir Patrick Neill, Vice-Chancellor of Oxford
University, reported to the Department of Trade and Industry on the
whole question of whether Lloyd's own self-regulatory measures provided the names with adequate protection.

In the event the Neill Committee gave little comfort either to the
hardline critics or to those who hoped that things might continue in the
old way. External supervision was ruled out—the new Council, Neill
decided, 'had transformed self-regulation at Lloyd's . . . We know of
no profession or equivalent organization which has accomplished such
a major programme of reform in such a short time-scale'.

But Neill urged several steps toward more stringent protection of
the outside members. The standard agency agreement made between
names and their underwriting agents, said Neill, was 'seriously defec-
tive' and there was still no adequate register of agents' charges. Lloyd's
should provide more information to prospective names about the per-
formance of individual agents, and there must be better arrangements
for compensating names against losses which arose 'otherwise than as
a result of the normal risks of underwriting'. An Ombudsman should
be created to deal with names' complaints, and there should be a
streamlined arbitration procedure to facilitate the investigation and
resolution of names' money claims against their agents. Mandatory
examinations—something which Lloyd's had perhaps not taken
seriously enough in the past—should be introduced for those intend-
ing to become active underwriters. Names should be protected, too,

from the consequences of the system of parallel or 'baby' syndicates set up by a minority of underwriters to cream off the most profitable business for themselves and favoured members. These, said Neill, were an 'evident abuse' and must be abolished within no more than two years from the Report's publication.

But Neill's most significant proposal was designed to reduce the influence of professional insiders in the running of the market. The balance of the twenty-eight strong Council, said the Report, should be changed in favour of the outside names by reducing the number of working members from sixteen to twelve. The number of non-working names on the Council would remain the same, but there would be eight instead of, as previously, four outsiders nominated by the Bank of England. Thus working names would be, for the first time, in a minority. The effective control of Lloyd's by insiders, which had existed since Angerstein's time, would be over.

It remains to be seen whether Neill's is the last word on Lloyd's, but at the time of writing, Lloyd's swift acceptance of his basic proposals seems a good omen for the future. The publication of the Report marked the end of one of the most turbulent periods that the market had ever seen—though it is worth remembering that everything at Lloyd's is writ large, whether scandals or successes.

'The only thing necessary for the triumph of evil,' said Edmund Burke, 'is for good men to do nothing,' and the market had paid a heavy price for its tolerance both of those who had exploited the system for their own ends, and of those who had let things slide, in the hope they would correct themselves, in the old easygoing manner. In the end, perhaps, the Lloyd's scandals were the most dramatic illustration possible of the moral climate of the times, when it seemed to some that money-making, by whatever means, had a higher priority than the integrity and tradition of the market.

7
'Report Me to Lloyd's'

IF you take the quiet by-lane that ascends from the ancient walls of Dover Castle, you will soon see what is perhaps the most stunning and historic coastal view in England. In the immediate foreground is the castle itself, and close to it the remains of the Roman lighthouse. In the middle distance lies Shakespeare Cliff, with the long tongue of Dungeness behind it. Out at sea coasters and supertankers move with slow deliberation down their sea-lanes, with Calais and Cap Gris Nez faint smudges in the distance.

Meanwhile the hill on which you stand, nearly four hundred feet above the Eastern Docks, has its own intriguing story. It is topped by an unusual white concrete building which could be said to resemble an eccentric mushroom. The reason for this is partly aesthetic, for the design reflects the curved shape of the nineteenth century gun emplacements that used to stand here. But there is also a practical reason for the building's wide curve, and the long windows giving sweeping views across the Channel: the Dover Straits Coastguard Station at Langdon Battery is the centre of search and rescue operations in the world's busiest marine highway. It ranks, Station Officer Mike Ford tells me with justifiable pride, with Falmouth as being the most modern and sophisticated of all the coastguard stations on our shoreline.

Station Officer Ford, a tall bearded man with a seagoing look about him, takes me into the big control room. The reason for the mushroom shape becomes clearer still, for the nerve-centre of the station is the great semi-circular desk that occupies it. It is always manned by a minimum of six—a senior watch officer, three or four regulars and one or two auxiliaries. If a vessel is in trouble, it will be their responsibility to call out the lifeboats from the North Foreland to Beachy Head, or to press the 'scramble' button for the Manston helicopters.

As we talk, one of the duty officers is on the phone to fishermen at Hastings. A drifting dinghy has been spotted five miles out at sea. 'Most likely,' says Mike Ford, 'it's adrift from a vessel. But we have to check, in case it might be an overnight fishing party where something's gone wrong.' Such things are the coastguards' bread-and-butter work, but sometimes their radios will crackle out a piece of world news. Only a week or so before, Mike Ford said, one of his officers had handled the distress message about the stricken Townsend Thoresen ferry that had tragically gone down off Zeebrugge. 'It was a seven-word message to say she was capsizing. It must have seemed almost unbelievable, but he kept his cool. Within seconds he'd put out a major disaster warning, and alerted the Sea-King helicopters that played a big part in the rescue.'

In the background the crackle of the radio goes on—coastguard station radios are tuned to VHF channel 16, which is the distress frequency all ships use. Having made contact, they will then turn to another frequency to leave it clear for distress messages.

'This is the *Westminsterbrook*. Calling Channel 16. Calling *Winchesterbrook*.' The auxiliary explains that they'll be sister-ships, wanting to get in touch with each other. There is a hum and a crackle and a polite Dutch voice saying good evening, he is Scheveningen Radio, and what frequency are they working on?

Mike Ford suggests we see the radar room, and on the way to it I notice a stack of *Lloyd's List* and some well-thumbed copies of Lloyd's other publications. Mike tells me he had worked himself at Lloyd's. In his youth, he had been a junior in the Underwriting Room, and then decided to go to sea. He had served for seven years in the Royal Navy, then after a spell in industry settled for the coastguard service, where he had a bit of both worlds. Contacts with Lloyd's, he said, were always cropping up—if the coastguards had a call-sign for a ship but not a name, it would be Lloyd's Intelligence Department they would turn to.

We move into the darkness of the radar room, where two regulars are intent upon their screens, on which the ships show as specks of light, like a maritime Milky Way. Over the next two years, says Mike Ford, they will be getting more up-to-date equipment—daylight-view radar which will mean they can get away from the darkened-room atmosphere and will be able to see a mirror-image of the radar through the window.

It is radar that enables the coastguards to control the traffic of the Channel. If a vessel moves out of its lane or breaks the keep-right rule, it will show on the screen, and a message to other ships in the area will be broadcast. Rogue vessels will be positively identified, usually by the Coastguard Islander aircraft. The evidence will then be passed to the government concerned to enable them to bring a prosecution.

One of the two operators begins talking on the radio, dictating a warning about a marker buoy that has broken adrift somewhere near Boulogne. 'Boulogne', he repeats, spelling it out. 'Bravo Oscar . . .'.

Back at the main control-desk, the watch officer is writing down the details of a motor yacht whose owner has just phoned in to say he is leaving Dover for Southampton, and will the coastguards note his destination and time of arrival. The question of the drifting dinghy seems to be resolved: Hastings has no knowledge of any parties that could have been in trouble. 'Confirmed broken adrift from a vessel as we thought,' says Mike Ford, in a relieved way. It is all part of the small change of shipping information, the constant stream of detail pouring out across a thousand crackling radios. How does it all relate to Lloyd's? To see that, we must go back to the earliest days of the coffee house.

'If anybody wants to know something about a ship or the sea, they come to us. To the ordinary person, Lloyd's means ships.'

These words, spoken by a Lloyd's agent in a West Country port, seemed to define what has come to be an almost unconscious connection: for two hundred years at least, Lloyd's has been regarded as the main source of all shipping information. Even in Edward Lloyd's time, *Lloyd's News* had been the main foundation of the coffee house's success. Though it ceased publication in 1697, Lloyd continued to issue shipping information whenever he had news of interest. Thus when the *News'* successor, *Lloyd's List*, appeared in 1734, there was a tradition to build on.

Even so, the actual published material was only the tip of the iceberg. By the end of the eighteenth century Lloyd's shipping knowledge was already regarded with awe in Whitehall. At least once in the Napoleonic Wars the Committee were able to give the Admiralty the first news that French ships had been sighted, off Cromer. When the British ship *Hopewell* was captured off Lowestoft in 1794—Lloyd's intelligence service seems to have been particularly efficient off the East Coast—they were able to inform the Admiralty, who in turn asked what convoy the *Hopewell* had sailed in. The Committee of Lloyd's, with due respect, told the Admiralty that she had not been in convoy at all, but they could give the name of the French vessel which had captured the *Hopewell*, not to mention from what port she had sailed and how many other British prizes she had taken.

In other ways Lloyd's had become recognized as an administrative power. If a naval captain wanted to complain of disobedience from merchant ships in convoy, he would contact Lloyd's rather than the Admiralty. Once, the Committee got to know of inadequate convoy arrangements at Falmouth. They passed the information to the First Lord, who dealt with it promptly. In the late 1790s, the relationship was such that Angerstein could write to the Admiralty Secretary to request that a ship of the line be stationed off Ostend, to protect the passage of a number of valuable merchantmen. By 1804, writes Angerstein's biographer, the coffee house was 'an empire within itself; an empire which, in point of commercial sway, variety of powers, and almost incalculable resources, gives law to the trading part of the universe'.

Meanwhile there had been one other event which would eventually lead to Lloyd's acquiring its most famous piece of hardware: the loss, in 1799, of the frigate *Lutine*. Originally launched at Brest in 1785, the *Lutine* had been one of sixteen French warships surrendered to Admiral Hood at Toulon in 1793. Her French name is roughly translatable as 'Sprite', but for some reason the British Navy, having acquired her, kept the French one. In her new role as HMS *Lutine* she was attached to the Mediterranean Fleet and was part of a frigate squadron under Nelson's command in 1794.

The *Lutine*'s next and most dramatic appearance in history came in 1799. In that year a number of British merchants in Hamburg found themselves pushed for credit as a result of the Napoleonic Wars. The London banks decided to send a cargo of bullion for their support, and asked the Admiralty to loan them a ship. The only one which happened to be available was the *Lutine* and she sailed from Yarmouth for Hamburg on 9 October under the command of Captain Lancelot Skynner. Included in her cargo there were nearly 42,000 Spanish silver *pistoles*, 58 bars of gold, and 81 double and 138 single gold *Louis*.

What happened then is an odd and slightly sinister story. For some reason, never discovered, she went off course. Around midnight on 9 October she struck the sands at the entrance to the Zuider Zee and sank in nine fathoms of water with the loss of all hands. Various theories have been put forward to account for why a ship bound for Hamburg should have gone aground in the Zuider Zee. There was, it is true, a north-westerly gale on the night in question. There are also stories of riotous celebrations among the officers before they left

Yarmouth, and even a mysterious rumour that the *Lutine* was secretly carrying the Dutch crown jewels.

Meanwhile the whole of her valuable cargo had been underwritten at Lloyd's, and the underwriters paid their losses promptly. The possibilities of salvage looked slight, since the Netherlands government claimed that the loss had been in their territorial waters. When, in 1801, a Dutch fisherman named Wyck brought up £83,000-worth of bullion, they claimed two-thirds, though they returned some silver spoons which had belonged to Captain Skynner to the dead man's father, and a sword made for the first lieutenant. It was identified by the mark of the maker, one Cullen, the King's cutler, of Charing Cross.

More attempts to raise the cargo came to little or nothing. There were protracted negotiations between Lloyd's and the Dutch government in 1814, 1821 and again in 1857. In 1859, divers working under the protection of a Dutch gunboat recovered £22,000-worth of bullion, the ship's bell and her rudder, which has since been carved into a chair and can be seen in the writing-room at Lloyd's.

The 80-lb bell itself, mounted on its wrought-iron frame, dominates the Room behind the Caller's rostrum. It is still possible to discern on it the date it was made, the crown and arms of the house of Bourbon, and also the inscription *St Jean*, which may have referred to the *Lutine*'s patron saint. Though its historic function of sounding the loss of a ship has virtually ceased, it is still the most famous visible symbol of Lloyd's.

As for the rest of the *Lutine* treasure, it was estimated in 1859 that a million pounds' worth of gold bars, Spanish *pistoles* and *Louis d'or* still lay buried beneath the shifting sands at the entrance to the Zuider Zee. Today, more than a century later, the *Lutine*'s golden treasure seems likely to remain there.

By the middle part of the nineteenth century there had been a considerable spread of Lloyd's 'almost incalculable resources'. It might be Lord Palmerston asking the Committee of Lloyd's to advise him how the British consul at Le Havre could recover nine guineas he had spent on helping the master of a schooner. It might be the Royal Society asking if Lloyd's could identify a curious bottle found in the River Ob in Siberia. (Lloyd's, with almost irritating expertise, was able to tell them that it was a device used by Norwegian fishermen as a float for their nets.)

Meanwhile in 1852 the Committee of Lloyd's had taken an important step to augment its communications service. It had begun to set up a chain of signal stations around the British coast. Partly this was to help underwriters, but it had a much wider use for merchants. In those days a ship might arrive from America or Australia without knowing which European port was currently paying the best price for her particular cargo. Thus the master of a British ship arriving in the Channel would signal her name and ask to be reported to Lloyd's. She would then lie off the coast, waiting for orders as to which port to proceed to.

The result was that Lloyd's signal stations became part of Britain's coastal landscape. If you walk to the top of Beachy Head today, you may sit on a bench enclosed by a low stone wall. On it, there is an inscription recording that it was originally part of a signal station belonging to Lloyd's of London. The people of the Lizard, writes Gibb, 'when they speak of Lloyd's, mean not the great building in Leadenhall Street but a little, squat, storm-beaten house on the cliff's edge which for half a century greeted English sailormen with their first welcome home'.

By 1883 the number of Lloyd's signal stations had grown to thirteen. By the end of the century it was nearly forty. Much of the expansion was due to Colonel Hozier, who as Secretary of Lloyd's had toured the coastline of England buying up land for the stations. Even so, by 1896 their day was almost over. In that year Marconi made his first radio transmission over nine miles, and signalling would soon be outmoded as a method of communication with ships at sea.

Of Hozier's original forty, only the one at Gibraltar still survives as a working signal station: ships entering the Mediterranean will still ask, in the old phrase, 'Report me to Lloyd's'. The Gibraltar station proved its continuing usefulness in the spring of 1973, when it helped to track a German vessel suspected of carrying arms for the IRA. The ship, thanks largely to the Gibraltar signal station's help, was eventually arrested on the coast of Ireland.

Meanwhile, since 1811, there had been another link in the chain of Lloyd's communications. This was the setting up of the system of agents. From the earliest days underwriters had had their own contacts in foreign ports who could help with the survey of ships and cargoes, but it had been a purely informal arrangement.

Now, since 1811, these informal contacts had been put on a more official basis. Underwriters wanting information about a ship or cargo in a foreign port would channel their queries through the local Lloyd's agent, who would also provide the market with information of sailings and arrivals.

By 1829, Lloyd's had appointed over 350 agents in the world's ports, mostly shipping brokers or traders whose day-to-day work would bring them in touch with shipping matters.

Today, movements in the world's ports are reported by Lloyd's agents back to Lime Street, and a million and a half of them a year will appear in the pages of *Lloyd's List*. The Intelligence Service has greatly grown, so that its world network of communications includes coast-guards, radio stations and sea-rescue posts in every country. Whether or not she is insured at Lloyd's hardly a move by any ship goes unrecorded.

Today, as always, Lloyd's means ships. More than ever today, it means their safety.

Roger Lowes, Casualty Reporting Officer at Colchester, has become an expert on one part of the world where, at the time of writing, ships are very unsafe. That is the tiny island of Kharg, at the top of the Per-sian Gulf, where the Iraqi air force has repeatedly bombed the world's oil tankers in an attempt to reduce Iranian exports. When you read or hear on television that another tanker has been hit by Iraqi exocets, it will almost certainly be Lowes who has given the details to the world's press.

Lowes operates from the Lloyd's of London Press building at Col-chester, where he sits in a small office surrounded with world maps divided into sectors. The morning I called on him had been, by his standards, only moderately hectic. He had come in as usual, at 7.50. Almost before he had had time to get himself a coffee from the vend-ing-machine, the phone had started ringing: one of his Middle Eastern sources, which he declined to name, had told him that a Greek tanker had been hit while loading at Kharg, and was believed to have been damaged or sunk.

Lowes' main contact for all Greek ships is the Ministry of Mercan-tile Marine at Piraeus. He had immediately contacted the naval com-mander on duty there, who promised to come back with further information. About 8.30 Lowes received a telex from Piraeus. The vessel concerned was the *Faroship L*, 138,255 tons gross, built in 1975 and owned by Ceres Hellenic Shipping Enterprises of Piraeus. The good news was that she had not after all, been hit, though three of her crewmen had been injured. But the loading quay had been destroyed by the missile, which sounded like bad news for underwriters.

Lloyd's Intelligence Department has become, for the world's press and for a host of safety services, the most comprehensive and authoritative bureau of shipping information. But the basic reason for its existence is to serve the interests of underwriters, so Lowes' first move was to transmit news of the incident by newswire to the Room, where it would immediately be posted on the casualty boards to greet underwriters arriving at their boxes after their morning conferences over coffee.

His next step was to inform each of the companies who pay an annual fee to the Intelligence Department to receive news of casualties in their area. Of 400 subscribers worldwide, 85 are in or around the Persian Gulf, and even though *Faroship L* was not in fact in need of help, this is an automatic service. 'There are always people hoping to make an honest bob out of ships in trouble,' says Lowes, whose client-list includes not only tug-owners, repair-yards and salvors, but airlines ready to repatriate crews to air-photo firms hoping to sell pictures of stricken vessels to the world's press. By 9.30 all subscribers in Sector B had been informed by computerized telex. As far as the Intelligence Department was concerned, the 241st bombing incident on Kharg was over.

Lowes accepts the semi-oracular status accorded him by the press with mild amusement. The week before I saw him, he had had a phone call from a TV station on the American east coast about another sinking in the Gulf. It hadn't been till he heard his questioner telling viewers 'we're now on a hot line to Lloyd's of London' that he realized he was talking live on a breakfast programme. Another time he was rung up by a ship's master while he was actually entering the Gulf. 'He kept asking me whether I thought it was safe for him to go in, then shouting "over!" I told him there was a risk, and it was up to him. He seemed to think Lloyd's ought to be able to predict things.'

It may seem unthinkable that a vessel of 2,000 tons could be lost in the busiest shipping lane in the world without trace or warning. But that is what happened to the Greek cargo ship *Gold Coin*. One December night she left Rotterdam, bound for Dakar with a cargo of maize. On the second night of her voyage she struck one of the worst gales ever recorded in the Channel, a night when even a naval officer, whose des-

troyer was bound for Chatham, recalled that his ship had practically
stood on end in the Straits.

No Channel boats had been able to cross that night, but next day the
morning ferry battered her way over from Boulogne. In mid-Channel
her master sighted what looked like a half-deflated life-raft. He
reported this to the Dover coastguards.

Ironically, the Dover coastguards knew nothing about the *Gold Coin*,
but were getting seriously worried about another vessel. This was the
Dutch coaster *Noblesse* which had been due in Dover Harbour early
that morning from the Port of London. A gang of dockers had been
engaged to unload her cargo from 8.00 a.m.

Two hours later there was still no sign of the *Noblesse*. The Dutch
owner's Dover agent had become worried and contacted the Dover
coastguards. They, in turn, sent a telex to the Port of London, only to
learn that the *Noblesse* had sailed at 10.00 p.m. the previous evening.

Thus as soon as they got the message from the master of the Channel ferry they immediately linked the floating life-raft with the *Noblesse*.
Obviously the next step was for the Dover coastguards to initiate a
search. Apart from sending out their own helicopter from Manston,
they also, as a matter of routine, got in touch with Lloyd's.

Would Lloyd's Intelligence initiate a broadcast enquiry? Within
minutes, the broadcast had gone out. Meanwhile Lloyd's, on their own
initiative, contacted the Rotterdam owners for a full description of the
ship, the colour of her hull, number of masts and funnel markings.
One coastguard explained to me that this can often be Lloyd's key role
in a search—to tell the searchers exactly what they are looking for. 'If
Lloyd's tell us she's got a crew of eight and we've picked up seven,' he
told me, 'then we know we've still got one more man to look for.'

But on that morning in the gale-swept Straits there was to be no
happy ending—almost at once the Manston helicopter reported seeing
four dead bodies on the life-raft. There was nothing to be done except
make what seemed a hopeless search for the rest of the crew. At
Dover, Station Officer William Barnes and another coastguard spent
the whole day scouring the beach and clifftop, looking for a sight of
wreckage. Meanwhile the lifeboat went out on its grim task of picking
up the four bodies from the life-raft.

Till now the Dover rescuers had been working on what seemed an
obvious conclusion—that the life-raft had belonged to the *Noblesse*.
But now something happened which threw an entirely new element
into the situation. The North Foreland coastal radio station had come

up with an answer to Lloyd's broadcast enquiry. The *Noblesse*, they said, was nowhere near the Dover Straits. She had sheltered from the gale almost immediately after leaving the Port of London, and was now lying safely at anchor in the Thames Estuary.

If there is one shaft of light in the whole dark story, it was the pleasure that Lloyd's could take in contacting the Dutch owners to tell them the *Noblesse* was safe. But meanwhile if the life-raft was not from the *Noblesse* what ship was it from?

By now Lloyd's had discovered something else, which was that during the night of the storm, the North Foreland radio station had heard what is known as an auto-alarm on their radio. Roughly an auto-alarm is a bit like a burglar alarm. On a small ship, the radio operator will have no relief, and yet must take occasional periods of rest. Before going below to get a sleep or a meal, he will switch on his auto-alarm. If any ship in the vicinity is sending out a distress message, his auto-alarm will send off a warning signal, a bit like the noise of a police car's siren, on frequency 2182. Coastguards and other ships will take it as a preliminary warning. All radio operators who hear it will immediately clear the frequency for a distress message.

The snag with the auto-alarm is that it can often be a false one—the Dover coastguard told me that they frequently get several bursts of auto-alarm in a day, because radio apparatus may be faulty. 'When a sparks is going below for a meal,' they explained, 'he switches on his auto-alarm and tests it. That means it'll go off for a few seconds, rather as you might test an alarm clock.'

Was this what happened with the auto-alarm heard by the North Foreland radio? Or was it a genuine distress signal, the only one ever given by the stricken *Gold Coin*?

Probably the true facts will never be known—but later it was found that the watches on the drowned sailors' wrists roughly tallied with the time when the auto-alarm had sounded. And the SOS had been preceded by the call-sign SXZB.

SX is the call-sign for a Greek vessel—the last two letters, ZB, should have denoted the name of the ship, but when Peter Bingham, of Lloyd's Intelligence, looked it up in the list of call-signs there was no ZB.

Lloyd's Intelligence Department began checking the movements of all Greek ships in the area. It took them all morning, before they eventually tracked her down as the *Gold Coin*. Even so, the clinching proof did not come till the Intelligence Department managed to contact the

Gold Coin's owners. Could they give Lloyd's the serial number of her life-rafts? They could, and it was identical with the one brought in at Dover.

All the resources of modern sea-rescue had not been enough to save the *Gold Coin*. Yet her story is not an entirely dark one, for it shows the interlocking pattern of communications which exists to save life at sea. In that pattern Lloyd's Intelligence plays a big part. Even when tragedy strikes, it can at least establish the facts. As a result of evidence given by Lloyd's Intelligence staff at the inquest on the *Gold Coin* victims, steps have been taken to tighten up world regulations concerning call-signs.

If casualty reporting is the sharp end of the Intelligence Department's work, shipping information is the bread-and-butter. 'Basically we are still doing what was done in Edward Lloyd's time,' says the ID's manager, Keith Bickmore. 'Telling underwriters that a ship has arrived at one port, or left it for another.' The difference, he goes on to explain, lies in the scale and detail of the information. Whereas the earliest existing copy of *Lloyd's List* records around eighty shipping movements, all from British and Irish ports, its modern counterpart fills three closely-printed pages of the paper.

Lists of shipping movements originate from Lloyd's agents' daily telexes from world ports. The Rotterdam area will have over 200 arrivals and departures in a day. Somewhere like Falmouth or Fécamp will have only half a dozen. The telexed lists of movements are handled by a staff of six shipping editors, whose job is to confirm and validate every movement, then punch it into the columns that will be printed in tomorrow's *Lloyd's List*. Every day at 3.15, the lists of the day's shipping movements are put on to magnetic tape and taken to the print-room where they are photographed in blocks of seven columns at a time. At 4.30 the same is done for Lloyd's other daily publication, the *Shipping Index*.

There are only two of Lloyd's of London Press's formidable range of papers. Among twenty or more others are the weekly *Voyage Record* and *Casualty Reports*, and a monthly list of laid-up vessels. *Lloyd's Loading List* and the *European Loading List* are weekly directories for exporters, telling them where they can find ships for their cargoes. Lloyd's of London Press also publishes its own law reports and Lloyd's Maritime Atlas, the world's most comprehensive nautical atlas for the shipping or insurance user. Other volumes indispensable to professionals are *Lloyd's Ports of the World* and *Lloyd's Maritime Directory* (larger than three London phone books, the latter lists details of 34,000 vessels).

But from the underwriter's point of view the most useful of all the publications is one that Lloyd's does not officially admit to at all. This hefty volume, known as the *Confidential Index*, comprises over 1,400 pages and is issued twice a year to subscribers only. 'It is a unique aid,' said one underwriter. 'Nowadays, for tax reasons, a ship is often registered as what we call a one-off, meaning that she's registered as a one-ship company. Only the *Confidential Index* will tell you who's the real owner, the year the ship was built, and his casualty record.' It may sound a bit like reading out a man's previous convictions in court, but few owners seem to mind. Shipowners who are sent proofs of the details relating to their ships invariably return them with, if necessary, corrections.

Lloyd's tradition as a news-gathering centre began, as we have seen, with Edward Lloyd. Many other publications are part of the tradition—the *Confidential Index*, for example, celebrated its centenary in 1985. But it is only very recently that all Lloyd's publications have been brought together under one roof. The modern Lloyd's of London Press is largely the creation of one man, Clifford Welch, who over the last fifteen years has become one of Lloyd's most formidable figures.

Sitting in the management offices overlooking the River Colne, Clifford Welch drew my attention to the handsome teak finish which is a feature of the Colchester headquarters. 'Just because it's a modern building we didn't want it to be all concrete and glass,' he says. 'The use of wood somehow exemplifies traditional values. And it's got the tang of the sea about it.'

It is the kind of thing, you feel, that matters to Clifford Welch, who manages to combine an immense workload with a rare ability to find time to discuss everyone else's interests. Later, sitting in one of the town's fish restaurants, he chatted about some of his own. They include boats, first editions, and the Royal Free Hospital at Hampstead, where he is a governor and an indefatigable fund-raiser.

But Clifford Welch's most passionate enthusiasm is reserved for Lloyd's. When he first became involved with it, he said, he had not known much more about the market than the next man. As a member of the board of IPC Business Press and chairman of the group's overseas publishing interests, his world was that of specialist technical magazines.

One day towards the end of 1972 he received a phone call out of the blue. It came from Paul Dixey, then Lloyd's Chairman. Would Clifford Welch come and have lunch to discuss a question on which, Dixey had heard, he might have the kind of expertise that Lloyd's was seeking?

Over the lunch Dixey explained the basic outline of the problem. Basically Lloyd's was disturbed that its publishing activities were losing money. *Lloyd's List*, with a world circulation of 10,000, was still required reading for most people to do with shipping. But the losses on the *List* and the other publications had recently been considerable—in some years touching £80,000. Could Welch, with his international reputation for making this kind of specialist publication pay, suggest a way of turning the losses into profits—while still maintaining the traditional standards?

A further series of meetings took place with, among others, Sir Henry Mance, Mervyn Herbert, who was advising the committee, and C. G. Wastell, Lloyd's Secretary-General. As the meetings went on Welch began to take in the daunting nature of the problem. The daily printing of *Lloyd's List*, varying from ten to twenty-four pages, was far from being the only item. Lloyd's was also committed to produce the *Shipping Index* of 200 pages a day, the *Voyage Record* of 240 pages a week, and the *Loading List*, also a weekly of 320 pages. It was, he realized, a bigger printing operation than faced even the biggest newspaper proprietor in the country—'the equivalent of updating and printing the Woking phone directory every day.' Nevertheless, when in March 1973 Lloyd's asked him formally to take over its newly-formed subsidiary, Lloyd's of London Press Ltd, under the chairmanship of Collwyn Sturge, then a member of the Committee, Welch decided to take on the job despite what would have been an enticing future at IPC. 'I was enthralled by the challenge of it,' he says simply.

By now the Committee of Lloyd's had decided on a specific target. They wanted to be sure that the publishing side could be made to break even within five years, and afterwards go into profit. Clifford Welch's answer was a five-year plan, whose basic feature was the computerization of the total information handling process, aimed to make the whole project far less labour-intensive than it had been: apart from editorial and printing staff there were, in 1973, over a hundred people solely engaged on plotting shipping movements.

But the computer was going to solve only half the problem. As a forward-looking publisher Welch knew that any thorough-going reform in the modern age would also involve the introduction of new methods. The drain on Lloyd's finances, he saw, could only be checked by the introduction of what most Fleet Street tycoons then saw only as a pipe-dream—computer-aided printing to replace the traditional typesetting methods which had remained not much altered since the time of Gutenberg. And if the new method was to be brought in, it would have to be outside London. There was no means by which the complex new equipment could be installed in the cramped basements of Lime Street—where *Lloyd's List* had been printed daily since the 1920s—while production was still going on in the old way.

Clifford Welch had already foreseen that relocation away from Lime Street would eventually, despite initial costs, mean considerable savings. But the cost, including the computer, software and redundancy payments, would be just on one and a quarter million pounds. Fourteen years ago it was a sum calculated to make many people in the market wince, but such was the Committee's faith in the project that in October 1973 they agreed that it should go ahead.

The next eighteen months saw the outline of the plan slowly but surely becoming real. The riverside site at Colchester was acquired, the computer and visual display units installed, the advanced printing equipment bought. Meanwhile the staff were trained to handle the new methods: by the end of September 1974 the whole printing operation was transferred to the new technology on schedule—with a reduction of more than a third in the total workforce. A year later the editorial offices were moved to temporary accommodation on the site while the new offices were being built. In 1976—which also saw the break-even point reached a year ahead of schedule—Lloyd's of London Press formally and proudly took possession of their building.

But recent changes in *Lloyd's List* are not merely the product of the computer. Today the *List*—it celebrated its 250th anniversary in 1984—has been modernized in style and format. It contains general news, and specialist pages on aviation, freight forwarding, offshore oil and general transport as well as shipping and insurance. Printed in two daily editions, the circulation has risen to over 15,000.

Lloyd's publications began with a single sheet of shipping movement news around the 1690s. Now, employing as advanced an information-handling and printing technique as any in the world, they have moved, as Clifford Welch puts it, 'beyond the constraints of the printed word.' The information originally brought by runner along some storm-swept cliffs to the nearest coach for London, is today no less romantically carried by space-shuttle.

Whatever the mode of communication—newspaper or databank—the information carried is likely to increase in importance. 'In the world equation of raw materials going one way and products the other, the biggest volume is still shipped in hulls,' says Clifford Welch. 'I don't see that equation changing.'

Lloyd's expertise in shipping intelligence is put to some diverse uses. One of the latest is the service provided by a new company called Lloyd's Maritime Information Service, which provides shipping news for the swarms of entrepreneurs who flock round ships like predatory seagulls. Those most obviously interested are the tug-owners and salvors anxious to clinch a deal with an owner or master of a ship in trouble, but there are many others. Ben Cotton, assistant manager of LMIS, told me that many of his clients are solicitors, who may be pursuing cases of marine fraud, or trying to locate a ship which has slipped out of some port without paying her dues. When she comes back into UK jurisdiction they would be in a position to arrest her. 'Then there are freight forwarders wanting to know when a ship will be in a particular port, or an exporter wanting to know if his cargo had been loaded. If an Arab owner is thinking of buying a particular ship, he might want to know if she'd traded with Israel. You get bunkering firms and people who're in the business of painting ships, and others who want to know when a tanker's arriving so they can try for a contract to clean out her oil tanks. There are even people who're in the business of buying wrecks. They sell them to Taiwan or Pakistani scrapyards.'

Last year fifty oil firms commissioned LMIS to provided them with a North Sea safety service. Under the system which the LMIS team devised, each of the oil firms has access to a computer databank which shows the names and current grid positions of both oil installations and fire-tenders in each sector of the North Sea. If anything goes wrong, the oil firm's managers have only to press a button on their video-screen to be immediately told the names, addresses and phone numbers of the emergency services they can call on.

All these services earn a handsome revenue for Lloyd's, but in the hard world of business one service is still run as a kindness. About ten phone calls a week come in from ships' captains' wives who can ring up to be told, without charge, the latest port their husband's ship is bound for. In the same way, the families of yachtsmen on long voyages are informed each time they are sighted. Few such lone travellers set out without the flag bearing the famous call-sign ZD2—'Report me to Lloyd's London'—so that passing ships will tell Lloyd's their position.

My final call was on deputy manager Dennis Kelley, who deals with police calls. If police in a West African country suspect a ship of smuggling drugs, they will want to know what other ports she may have been to. The previous week, Mr Kelley had had a call from Scotland Yard, who were investigating a murder in London's Chinatown. The request was for information about new arrivals from the Far East, on which the murderer might have landed. That morning, he said, he had been trying to help a client who was looking for what you might call a needle in a haystack. 'This client's £¼m trimaran had been run down in the Thames estuary in the middle of the night. All he knew about the running-down ship was that she must be painted dark green, because there was a scrape of green paint on the top of the trimaran's mast which had been shattered. He guessed that since it was in the estuary, she must have been heading for some east coast port, and he wanted a list of vessels that might have been around the area at the time. We gave him a print-out of over 100 possible vessels. The last I saw of him, he was going off with his print-out to hire an aeroplane to try to find her.'

'Gum arabic.' Captain Downs, who works for the Lloyd's agent at Hull, picked up the piece of yellow, rather quartz-like substance and tapped it on his desk. 'It's the stuff they put in fruit gums. Doesn't taste of anything itself, but it does when they melt it down and flavour it.'

I sniffed the hard yellow substance and handed it back. What, I asked, had gum arabic to do with being a Lloyd's agent?

He grinned and said there was practically nothing that didn't sooner or later come the way of Lloyd's agents. It might be somebody ringing up in the middle of the night to say there was a floating log in the Humber, or it might be a lady who had lost track of her son who was at sea and thought Lloyd's would be able to help her find him. 'As a matter of fact,' he added as an afterthought, 'we usually can.'

Meanwhile he wouldn't be surprised if there were one or two calls this morning—it had been foggy in the river since dawn, and now by midday it was getting worse. They got most sorts of bad weather in Hull including fog: one of the local sayings was that down by the river you could shovel it.

Captain Alan Downs was at sea himself for thirteen years till he came to this job. The firm he works for now is called Brown Atkinson. One of the oldest-established ship brokers in Hull, they have been Lloyd's agents, according to the placque in his office, since 1857.

'In those days the firm used to run a fleet of whalers of their own.' He looked up rather nostalgically at the pictures of ships on the wall. Brown Atkinson's looks as you feel a shipping office should—huge old-fashioned desks and a picture of King Haakon on the wall of the outer office because Mr Fenton, the managing director, is also the Norwegian consul.

Although his door is marked 'Surveyor', Captain Downs explained that he looks after everything to do with the Lloyd's agency side of the business. This means he covers an area from Flamborough to the south bank of the Humber. There are also a couple of sub-agents at Goole and Bridlington, whose job is mostly reporting casualties and shipping movements. When he sends in his daily telex list of shipping movements to Colchester, these will be included, though the greater part will be from the port of Hull itself.

If there are casualties, Captain Downs will usually hear of them through the local tug-owning firm—though in general terms, he said, an agent isn't likely to be one of the earliest sources of casualty news. The sort of thing where he did help was when the Intelligence Department had lost track of a ship. He had sent a telex only that morning about a ship which had sailed for Hull from Tynemouth nearly a fortnight before. The Intelligence Department had been worried when she hadn't been reported as arriving at Hull—he had made a few enquiries and found that in fact she had gone straight to dry-dock, which meant that she wouldn't have been reported as an arrival in the usual way.

Otherwise Captain Downs's main job is surveying casualties. Mostly this means cargoes—in the case of damage to ships themselves, he said, Lloyd's agents both at home and abroad would call in a marine surveyor. What Captain Downs does do is to see a cargo on which there may be a claim. If a fire breaks out in the ship's hold, the consignee of the cargo will get in touch with him as Lloyd's agent, and ask him to assess the damage.

Captain Downs stressed that it is not part of his job to get involved in liability, but simply to get a survey done efficiently and quickly. 'We haven't seen the policy and we don't want to see it. If we did, it wouldn't be so easy to be impartial.'

Apart from fires in the hold, I asked, what sort of cargoes did things go wrong with?

He said the difficulty was to think of a cargo which didn't have things go wrong with it. Once he had had to survey a lot of tinned pineapples that had been loaded in Singapore, and by the time they had got to Hull, they'd been cooked. 'When we opened the tins the juice had begun to ferment and the fruit was brown. The trouble was they'd been stowed too close to the boilers.'

One of the first jobs he had ever had was to meet a man who was an importer in the wholesale food business. He had imported a cargo of liver sausage from Germany, and insured it with a German company who had appointed Lloyd's agent to represent them in the case of a query.

'By the time it got to Hull,' recalled Captain Downs, 'there was more than a query. The sausage had gone all mouldy, with a sort of fur sticking to it. The Port Health people wouldn't let him sell it, even if anyone would have bought it, so they asked me to go along and see it. I suppose being new to the job I let him talk me into it, but I agreed to go back and see him next day. When I got there it was all beautiful—he'd taken it home and cleaned it and sprinkled French chalk on it. We didn't let him get away with it, but the point was he knew the German insurers wouldn't pay up. He'd told them he was going to transport the cargo in cold storage, but he hadn't. He'd let it go as ordinary cargo because he didn't want to pay the extra.'

How often, I asked, was an agent able to save the underwriters money? Captain Downs said it wasn't primarily what an agent was there for, but it happened quite often. 'That bit of gum arabic I showed you just now—that was part of the cargo that came here from Port Sudan. When it got to the wharf it smelt of mothballs, so we had it tested by chemists. It had been contaminated by naphthalene gas.'

I wondered how naphthalene gas could have got into gum arabic, and Captain Downs grinned. They'd had quite a job finding that out, he said, till he had discovered that the gum arabic had been stowed near some Ethiopian hides, which were being imported to make handbags. 'I'd dealt a good deal in hides at one time, for a local tanner and I remembered reading something about Abyssinian sheepskin. When I looked it up in *Lloyd's Survey Handbook* it said Abyssinian rawhides were always prepared for shipment with naphthalene as a protection against vermin.'

Even so, Captain Downs added, that hadn't solved the problem, though it was a good example of how an agent had to be a bit of a detective. Meanwhile he had still been stuck with 3,000 bags of gum arabic that smelt of mothballs. What he had done was to rent a warehouse and ventilate the bags by stacking them separately and leaving all the doors of the warehouse open. In the end they'd got rid of the smell and the chemists had pronounced the cargo free of naphthalene. It had been a fairly rough-and-ready method but it had saved the underwriters a lot of money.

On the other hand there were quite a lot of cases where you could only get a small proportion of salvage money back for the underwriter—would I like to see the *Marbella*, a trawler that had come in two days ago with a cargo that was going to have to be used as fishmeal? Most of the shipment had been taken out of her holds by now, but they would still be working on her—provided we could see anything—at the Hull Fish Quay.

We got in his car and drove through the fog that was circling the cold air like smoke from a bonfire. When we got down to the dock it was even thicker. The bow of the trawler loomed out, a dim blur of light coming from the sort of gantry they have at football grounds. On her decks you could see everything covered with reddish rust, great lengths of steel hawser and floats the size of beach balls.

'They've been through a hell of a time,' said Captain Downs. 'Twenty-six men for ten weeks, and all they've brought back is what amounts to a load of manure.' What had happened, he explained, was that the *Marbella* had struck a hurricane off the coast of Newfoundland. The ship had rolled so badly that the cargo of deep-frozen fish had broken the wooden boarding at the sides of the hold. Once the boarding had gone there had been nothing to protect the refrigeration pipes—either the wood or the frozen slabs of fish had fractured the pipe and there had been a burst.

'The stuff in the refrigeration pipes is tricoethylene, which is like dry-cleaning fluid. Of course it leaked, and contaminated the fish.' As a result, all the 220 tons of fish had been condemned. All Captain Downs could do now was arrange for the Ministry expert to see it, and agree that it should be sold for fishmeal to reduce the claim.

While Captain Downs was explaining, the fish were still coming out from the holds on the canvas conveyor, tucked in wallets like a cartridge belt. On the dockside the bobbers, as Hull fish porters are known, were loading them into crates. One of the frozen slabs fell on the ground and bounced as if it had been a cricket bat. Captain Downs picked it up—there must have been fifteen or twenty cod or pink bream frozen together in the slab, their eyes popping out like buttons.

'You can see that yellow stain along the side. That's been left by the tricoethylene.' Even in the icy air of the dockside, you could smell it.

Presently we went up on the deck and picked our way over the fishing gear. The way to the hold was down a long steel ladder. At the top one of the bobbers pushed back his red woollen cap and said I'd better borrow his gauntlets. 'You'll need to be careful where you put your feet down there.' I looked down closer into the hold. There must have still been fifty tons of fish, the slabs lying aslant each other like frozen see-saws.

'You can imagine what it was like down here in a Force Twelve.' The bobber who had lent me his gloves followed me down, shifting a slab of fish with the hook all bobbers carry, like some primitive surgical aid, because there is no other way of shifting fish. 'Catfish,' he said, looking it in the eye. 'That's a tasty fish.'

We slid precariously across the see-saws of fish to the side—in the refrigeration pipe there was a tiny gash, about the size of a fingernail. It was that which had caused the damage, said Captain Downs—that little nick in the pipe had cost the underwriters £40,000.

'At least there's one good thing,' said Captain Downs as we left. 'The crew are paid by contract. They won't lose by it.'

If the Lloyd's agent at Hull deals in anything from gum arabic to salami and Abyssinian rawhides, what about those in more exotic ports? Lloyd's has four hundred principal agents abroad, as well as another six hundred sub-agents. In addition to intelligence and survey work, a foreign agent will also have to settle claims on behalf of the underwriter. Lloyd's world-wide reputation is such that any bank from Nice to Nicaragua will honour what is called a Lloyd's 'sight draft'. Issued by the agent on the spot, the draft, as its name implies, will be paid promptly to the insured person.

Lloyd's agents do not receive a salary. Like those at Hull, most work for Lloyd's as an incidental to their main business as general shipping agents. In most cases they are expected to provide the shipping intelligence free. Surveys and claims are paid for on a scale basis.

Beyond his run-of-the-mill work a Lloyd's agent will also be expected to provide the kind of political background material which could be of use to underwriters. It may be a port where some corrupt official is turning a blind eye to the fact that cargoes are being pushed into the sea, then claimed on, or it may be a strike in South America which could affect contingency business. If an underwriter has to pay for delays, then it is in his interest to know if there might be a strike. Information of this kind is noted in something about which Lloyd's tends to be reticent, the Pink Sheets, which go to all marine underwriters in the Room, as well as to outside subscribers, and are marked Confidential.

Sometimes an agent may find himself unexpectedly involved in police work. One day an Englishwoman who had been living in the West Indies came into the Intelligence Department to ask if they could help trace her husband who had gone off cruising in his yacht with another woman—somewhere, she thought, down the west coast of Africa. The Intelligence Department prides itself on always trying to help, even on the scantiest information. In he course of their enquiries they found that the husband was wanted by Interpol.

'It seemed they'd been looking for him for months,' says the Intelligence Department with modest pride, 'and we found him in two weeks. Once we knew the South African police were looking for him, we guessed he'd have made for South America. The closest point in South America to the African coast is a place called Fortaleza, so we sent a telegram to our agent there. He sent us back a reply immediately—both the yacht and the man were there.'

Another time the Devon police asked Lloyd's if they could trace a yacht called the *Angelique* that had been reported missing from Brixham. There was no sign of any vessel of that name in *Lloyd's List*, but one day somebody in the Intelligence Department noticed that another yacht, the *Astrolabe*, had just arrived at Corunna. It occurred to him that the first and last letters were the same, and that the number of letters between them fitted. So, when he looked it up, did the tonnage. The result was the arrest of the yacht-thieves within hours.

But perhaps the oddest story of a yacht recovery came when Mr O'Keefe, the Lloyd's agent at Bantry in Ireland, happened to notice a yacht called the *Lis* coming into the small—and as it turned out, aptly named—harbour of Crookhaven in Galway. Because the arrival of any new craft there was unusual, he went on board and met the owner. Meanwhile a local freelance photographer also took a picture of the *Lis*.

It appeared in a Cork newspaper, and also found its way to a London newspaper office. Here it happened to be seen by somebody who was interested in boats, and who remembered having read about a yacht called the *Melisse* which had been stolen from the Hamble River near Southampton. He got in touch with Lloyd's, who instructed Mr O'Keefe to return to Crookhaven. Closer inspection by the Lloyd's agent showed that the name had been painted out except for the three central letters. In the end it was those three letters which led to the yacht's recovery.

At Lloyd's everything comes back to the Room. And if there is one image of Lloyd's more evocative than anything else, it is the sight of underwriters' clerks copying down their notes from the Casualty Boards. It is the point where the world of business meets the sea, the world of rusty coasters and kerosene drums and Force Nine gales. It is where an excess-of-loss policy has something to do with four drowned sailors on a life-raft.

The news posted on the Casualty Boards may be anything from the loss of a jet airliner to a small fire in a coaster's hold—if it is a casualty, it will go on the Board. The notice itself will have been telexed up from Colchester, photocopied, then placed on the Boards—yellow for marine casualties, which are known as yellow perils, pink for non-marine and blue for aviation.

One member of the ID staff has the job—almost as time-honoured as the Caller's—of writing in Lloyd's legendary Loss Book. 'Although it is traditionally known as the Loss Book, it is really a casualty book,' explained David Burling, the present Loss Book Clerk. 'Only about one per cent of the yellow perils are ever entered in the Book—those which are either expensive or a potential loss.'

Although its early volumes are among the treasures of Lloyd's, Burling said that the Loss Book on its lectern is not simply a picturesque survival. The point of putting a loss on record in the Book is that underwriters will have it brought to their attention.

'The clerks,' he said, 'will see me writing, then come over to see the name of the ship that's lost. They'll copy down details of what I've put in the Book—then go back to their boxes and look up their records to see if they've got a line on her.' Besides actually writing in the Book, the Clerk's job is to gather information for the Intelligence Department from the Room. If there is an overdue, for example, the brokers may have been given news by the owner, and Burling's central position makes him an ideal ear for information. The view from his desk is perhaps the best in Lloyd's. Immediately in front of it stands the massive oak rostrum designed by Sir Edwin Cooper for the 1928 Room, from which hangs the Lutine bell, while far above it is the great atrium which is the centrepiece of the architect's design.

What, I asked, about the Bell? Didn't recording a casualty also involve the sounding of Lloyd's most historic symbol?

Nowadays, Burling said regretfully, it didn't. Most people supposed the bell was rung every time there was a loss, but this no longer happened. On the rare occasions when the Bell is still sounded, its purpose is to stop dealings in the overdue market. This means that when a vessel is overdue, Burling's job is to find out at what reinsurance rate it is being written in the Room. The fears for the ship will be reflected in the amount of premium which the underwriter has to pay to reduce his commitment.

If the rate goes beyond a certain point, then Lloyd's rule is that the Bell must be rung as soon as there is news of the ship; if the news is given to the whole market at once, then no underwriter can have the advantage of special knowledge (as, for instance, Samuel Pepys had over the vessel described on page 13. One marine underwriter pointed out to me that this was a good example of the kind of thing the ringing of the Bell is designed to prevent).

With modern communications the need seldom, in any case, arises. David Burling told me the Bell had only been rung twice in the new Room—once for its formal opening and again in November 1986 when the Queen came. The last time it had been rung for an actual overdue had been on 10 November 1981 for a vessel named the *Gloria* which had been overdue at Hampton Roads, on a voyage from Houston to Famagusta.

Presently he said it was time for him to draw the line. At four-thirty every afternoon he rules a ritual red line under the day's losses with one of the quill pens he gets from the swannery at Abbotsbury in Dorset. Swans, it seems, are decreasing in the British Isles, so Burling is trying to build up Lloyd's stock. 'I go down to the swannery regularly,' he says, 'at the end of summer when the swans moult. The swanherd usually has about 150 for me. At the rate of one a fortnight, that should last a good time.'

The world loves a story of courage: consider that of Captain Christoforos Kakkaris, master of the tanker *Kymo*. On a winter afternoon the *Kymo* was bound from the East Indies to Japan with a cargo of resin and fuel oil, when there was an explosion amidships which set fire to the bridge and the officers' quarters.

Within ten minutes the crew were safely away in the boats, but not Captain Kakkaris. He jumped from the blazing bridge, managed to drop the port anchor, then tried to get through the blazing afterpart. Because of the fire he could not reach it, so he dived overboard and swam back to the stern. With the help of the Chief Engineer and three crew members, he fought the fire and brought it under control, three times refusing to leave his ship.

Some months later Captain Kakkaris received a unique reward for his courage. It was announced that, as well as a cash award, he was to be given Lloyd's Silver Medal which is only given for extreme heroism at sea. The other crew members who had helped him were also awarded medals. In making the award to Captain Kakkaris, the Committee were carrying on one of their oldest traditions—the idea that because Lloyd's insures ships, it has an obligation to those who risk their lives in them.

The first tangible expression of this sense of obligation goes back to 1782 when the members of Lloyd's raised £2,000 for the dependants of seamen lost in the *Royal George*. Possibly *The Times* overstated the case a little when it described the Committee of Lloyd's as 'the father of every seaman's orphan'. Even so, in those days when there was no kind of state help for those disabled in war or for their dependants, it was a beginning.

It was not until the Napoleonic Wars that Lloyd's charitable effort began in earnest. In 1794, after the Glorious First of June, a series of funds was begun to help those wounded in particular battles. The fund for the Glorious First of June raised £21,000. Then, in 1798, came the Battle of the Nile. It was a victory which touched Lloyd's underwriters' pockets as well as their patriotism. Because of it, British merchantmen could now sail unmolested through the Mediterranean.

The members of Lloyd's showed their gratitude to the tune of nearly £40,000. All sailors who lost a leg or an arm in the battle got £40. Nelson himself, we might feel a little disproportionately, was voted £500 to buy a silver dinner service, which he duly ordered from Rundall & Bridge, the City silversmiths.

Although there is no actual record of the presentation, it seems likely it took place on 15 November 1801, when he was reported in *The Times* as 'having been upon the Royal Exchange some time'. Six months later, after the Copenhagen fund was raised, he seems to have planned to visit Lloyd's again, for he wrote to Angerstein: 'I feel—and I am certain every Officer and man in the Fleet does the same—much indebted to the Gentlemen of the Committee for the attention they pay, and trouble they experience, on this occasion. I hope in a few days to have it in my power to pay my respects personally to them.'

Meanwhile the more general fund-raising was still going on, and in 1803 a Meeting of Lloyd's Subscribers was held to inaugurate what was to be called the Patriotic Fund. This was to be a campaign on a national scale, based on Lloyd's as today such fund-raising is based on the Mansion House. Like the previous Lloyd's funds, its objects were to help the wounded and their dependants, or as the Committee rather dramatically put it:

To animate the efforts of our Defenders by Sea and Land, . . . for the purpose of assuaging the anguish of their Wounds, or palliating in some degree the more weighty misfortune of the loss of Limbs—of alleviating the Distresses of the Widow and Orphan—of soothing the brow of Sorrow for the fall of their dearest Relatives, the props of unhappy Indigence or helpless Age . . . the Mite of the Labourer combining with the Munificent Donation of the Noble and Wealthy shall be the best pledge of our Unanimity.

The Committee's prose style may have been a little carried away, but there was no doubt of the campaign's success. The City companies and other insurance offices contributed their thousands and the Labourers, as the Committee had hopefully anticipated, their Mites. Three watermen of Shadwell Docks sent £5. Theatres gave the proceeds of special performances; the Bank of England and the East India Company gave £5,000 each.

Apart from the more general charitable purposes, much of the money went, as before, on presentations. After Trafalgar the recipients included all Nelson's captains, who were each given a silver cup designed by Flaxman. Lady Nelson was given plate, and so was Commodore Dance, who had beaten off a French squadron with his fleet of East Indiamen.

Curiously, it does not seem to have occurred to the Committee of Lloyd's that it might be a shade presumptuous to set up what was really a sort of private Honours List. Probably they did not take much notice of the radical journalist William Cobbett, who objected to what he called 'a set of traders at Lloyd's' usurping the function of the Crown by awarding honours. But when they presented a silver vase to Sir Home Popham for his expedition to Buenos Aires, it was too much even for the Admiralty. Popham's adventure had turned out a disaster and he was court-martialled. The First Lord described the Patriotic

Fund as 'that mischievous system of awards administered by the Committee of Lloyd's'. In 1809, ostensibly at least because of the calls on the Fund arising from the heavy casualty lists in the Peninsular War, the presentations were tactfully abandoned.

Over the years a good deal of the great dinner service presented to Nelson has been bought back. Today it forms the centrepiece of what is known as the Nelson Collection. In it you may see Nelson's Order of the Bath, various letters to Angerstein and the Log Book of the *Euryalus*, which as the signal-repeating frigate at Trafalgar recorded Nelson's most famous signal during the battle. As to the dinner service itself, it has been kept lovingly through the years, not least by Nelson himself who often referred to it with pride, and had a special sea-chest made to take it. Since its return to Lloyd's it has only been once used—at a dinner given by the Committee in 1948 to honour Sir Winston Churchill.

Meanwhile there have been many less ostentatious ways, over the centuries, in which Lloyd's has shown its sense of obligation. One of the outstanding instances was the help it gave to Henry Greathead, who is often credited with the invention of the life-boat. The story is so odd, adventurous and inextricably linked with Lloyd's that it is worth telling in a little detail.

Wind-swept and sea-fretted, the small grey town of South Shields lies on the Durham bank of the Tyne, guarded by a traditionally perilous group of rocks called the Black Middens.

It is known as a clannish place. The craft of pilotage in the harbour entry is still handed down from father to son. 'Arl tiggither like the folks of Shields' has long been the popular saying. Even today there is a hint that somebody from Newcastle or Darlington is a little foreign.

The clannishness may be one reason why South Shields people have only a grudging pride in Henry Greathead. Originally born at Richmond in Yorkshire, he came to Shields as a boy and learned his trade there as a ship's carpenter. In 1779 he was on a ship bound from the Tyne to Grenada. A few days out of port, he discovered that the ship's master planned to wreck her on the Goodwins to get the insurance money. With the aid of some of the rest of the crew, Greathead managed to prevent the captain's design, but could not stop him running the ship aground off Calais later. The captain then went to the port authorities at Calais, swore an affidavit that the ship had gone aground because of bad weather, and called his crew to sign it with him.

Greathead not only refused to sign the affidavit, but got several of the rest of the crew members to refuse as well. On his return to London he went to Lloyd's and told them the true story. He met several of the underwriters, among them one named James Forsyth, and another named Peter Warren who was a partner of Angerstein's. Thanks to the information he gave, they were able to refuse the owner's claim.

All this was the mere prologue to Greathead's later adventures. From now on his experiences read like something in a boy's adventure story. He was captured by American privateers in the Caribbean, offered a commission in the American Navy, and twice press-ganged by the British. Continuing to behave like a hero of fiction, he returned home in 1783 to South Shields to marry the humble girl he had always loved. But Greathead had one other ambition.

All his life—and after his adventures no one could have been more aware of the need—he had been working on a plan for what he called a safety-boat or life-boat. He got back to Shields, settled to a boat-building business, and in his spare time began work on the life-boat.

Before long, however, he became faced with that perennial problem for inventors, a shortage of cash. He began to think around the problem and remembered Lloyd's. Now that he needed help to complete his designs, who better to approach than the underwriters he had himself helped, four years earlier? He wrote to Forsyth and Warren, enclosing his drawings. True to the storybook pattern of Greathead's life, the Lloyd's underwriters did not merely write back praising Greathead's designs; they sent money, and an introduction to the Duke of Northumberland, who visited Greathead's workshop.

It is at this point that the fictional element ends in Greathead's life and a more human note of conflict enters. Curiously there was another local man working on the idea of a life-boat—or perhaps it is not so curious if you stand even today on Beacon Hill at Shields, listening to the gong-like sounds of the buoys, looking out to the Black Middens from the site where the local people used to light beacons to guide in shipwrecked sailors.

The name of the rival inventor was the unlikely one of Willie Wouldhave, and he was in every way Greathead's opposite. As Greathead was clearly urbane, practical and efficient, so Wouldhave seems to have been sour, eccentric and possessed of an explosive temper. Born in Liddle Street, North Shields in 1751, he had turned his hand to building clocks, electrical apparatus and organs as well as life-boats. Almost the archetypal figure of the inventor, his pictures show him as having the harrowed, elongated features of an El Greco portrait.

When Wouldhave began work on designing a life-boat is not clear, but one local legend of him is not unworthy of comparison with the insight of a Fleming or a Newton. One day, it is said, he went to the local well to get a drink. There was a woman drawing water at the well, and she asked him to help her with her skeel—the traditional local name for a pail of water.

Floating in the water in her skeel was a piece of broken wooden dish or scoop—presumably it was something like the shape of a slice of melon, for Wouldhave noticed that it floated with the points upward. However it was dropped in the water, it righted itself. Wouldhave went home, and from that day began to think in terms of a design which would right itself, as the piece of broken scoop had done, in the roughest water.

Meanwhile, in the late 1780s, there had been a long chain of ship-wrecks off South Shields. These had reached their climax in the wreck, in September 1789, of a ship called the *Adventure* which had gone aground with heavy loss of life. Public opinion in South Shields had been so appalled by this succession of disasters that it was decided to hold a competition for a life-boat. A committee was formed by a local society called the Gentlemen of the Lawe-House. Somewhere in the latter end of 1789 it met to consider the rival designs, under the chairmanship of one Nicholas Fairless.

How many other designs there were besides those of Greathead and Wouldhave we do not know—but we do know that they both entered. Greathead's was long and flat, with no buoyancy from cork or airboxes.

Wouldhave's, by contrast, had a high prow and stern, like the piece of broken scoop he had seen floating in the woman's skeel. At both ends there were watertight cases containing cork for extra buoyancy, and there was more cork along the floor. The model itself was twenty-two feet long and made of tin. Its other feature was that it had what boat-builders call a sheer—a cutaway, slanting shape to the sides of the hull.

Whatever the committee thought of the models, the personal impression made by Wouldhave was disastrous. Asked by Nicholas Fairless what advantage it had over its rivals, Wouldhave is said to have turned angrily upon him. 'Why, I say it will neither sink nor go to pieces nor lie bottom up. Will any of yours do as much?'

Perhaps it was a question the committee did not care to answer. They decided that neither design was suitable, but that Wouldhave should be awarded one guinea by way of compensation for his efforts. Even in those days the prize must have seemed derisory, and Wouldhave refused it with contempt.

What could the Gentlemen of the Lawe-House do? In the manner of committees, they decided on a compromise. It was arranged that Fairless and the more amenable Greathead should combine their efforts— Fairless presumably merely holding a watching brief on behalf of the committee. But the design they should work on would incorporate Wouldhave's essential features of the high prow and stern, as well as the cork for buoyancy.

Greathead and Fairless must have worked fast. Between the loss of the *Adventure* which had inspired the competition and the actual launching, there was a period of only four months. First Greathead made a clay model. It was like Wouldhave's tin one, but it contained the important new feature of having a cambered keel instead of a straight one. The model was inspected and approved, and Greathead was commissioned to build the boat at a cost of £91.

Thirty feet long and built to carry a crew of ten, she was launched on 31 January 1790, and named, perhaps a little ambiguously, the *Original*. The date of her first rescue is obscure, but evidently proved the life-boat's worth. It was of seven men who were rescued from the sloop *Edinburgh* in a sea 'so monstrous that no other boat could have lived in it'.

Over the next twelve years Greathead's boatyard appears to have flourished. He built twenty-one life-boats, including one to the Duke of Northumberland's order for the neighbouring seaport town of North Shields. His own fame began to spread and was even celebrated in verse, as in the 'Ode addressed to Mr Greathead the Inventor by Dr Trotter, Physician to the Fleet':

> 'A gift beyond the poet's flame,
> A grateful crew shall incense burn,
> And GREATHEAD shine in deathless fame,
> While love and friendship hail the tar's return!'

Even so, there was an unending need for funds. When Greathead appealed to the House of Commons in 1801, the House was too involved with the Napoleonic Wars to spend money on life-boats. It was left to Lloyd's, in the following year, to make far the largest contribution that had yet been made to the life-boat service. On 20 May 1802, on Angerstein's initiative, the underwriters of Lloyd's voted £2,000 'for the encouragement of life-boats being instituted in different parts of the coast of this kingdom'. The immediate result was the building of fourteen life-boats for coastal towns from Lowestoft to Fishguard and Newhaven to Arbroath. The more far-reaching result was the setting up, in 1824, of the National Life-boat Institution, the forerunner of the present RNLI.

Meanwhile in South Shields they still argue about who actually invented the life-boat. Wouldhave died in poverty in 1821 and was buried in the churchyard of St Hilda's, the stone eighteenth-century church which dominates the town and looks towards the Bergen and Oslo quays. Today a stone commemorates him as the inventor of 'that blessing to mankind, the life-boat'. Certainly much of the evidence seems to support the claim. Even apart from the story of the skeel, there is something dark and flickering in what we know of his character that suggests the true inventor.

On the other hand an idea is often produced as much by a climate of inventive thought as by an individual; perhaps a truer perspective would show Wouldhave as the lonely genius, but Greathead as the practical man who, seeing the importance of actually getting the life-boat built, had the good sense not to offend the committee that proposed to build it.

Ultimately any great project needs both aspects, and both are commemorated on a single monument that stands today near the seafront at South Shields. Built in 1890, it bears the names and carved faces of both men. Next to it stands their true memorial—the South Shields life-boat *Tyne*, which between 1833 and 1890 saved over 1,000 lives.

Today, as always through its three hundred years of history, Lloyd's means ships. 'We are all obliged by your humane attention to us seamen,' wrote Nelson to Angerstein once, identifying himself as always with the humblest.

Today, though it may take different forms, the attention to seamen is still there. It may be a weekly phone call for a captain's wife, or it may be the total resources of the Intelligence Department brought into play to help a vessel in danger. It may be a medal for a Greek sailor, or hours of time-consuming research to give pleasure to some small boy or old sailor who writes in to ask if Lloyd's can help him identify a ship.

In the end it is the quality which sets Lloyd's apart—the extra dimension of service.

LLOYD's LIST. N° 560

FRIDAY, January 2. 1740.

THIS List, which was formerly publish'd once a Week, will now continue to be publish'd every *Tuesday* and *Friday*, with the Addition of the Stocks Course of Exchange, &c.——Subscriptions are taken in at Three Shillings per Quarter, at the Bar of *Lloyd*'s Coffee-House in *Lombard-Street*.

Such Gentlemen as are willing to encourage this Undertaking, shall have them carefully deliver'd according to their Directions.

London *Exchanges* on	
Amst.	34 11 a 10
Ditto Sight	34 7½ a 8
Rott.	35 a 1
Antw.	35 11 a 36
Hamb:	33 10 2U a 11 2½
Paris —	32¼
Ditto at 2U	32⅜
Bourdeaux Usance	32¼
Cadiz —	42¼
Madrid	42⅜
Bilboa	41¼
Leghorn	51¼
Genoa	55
Venice	51¾
Lisbon	5 4⅞ a 5
Oporto	5 4½
Dublin	8

Aids in the Exchequer		*Given for*	*Paid off*
18th 2 Shilling	1739	1000000	926800
18th 4 Ditto	1740	2000000	482600
Malt——	1739	750000	501014
Salt——	1734	1000000	910500

Gold in Coin - - - -		3	18	1
Ditto in Barrs - - -		3	18	
Ps of Eight Pillar large - - -	per Oz	0	5	7½
Ditto Small - -		0	5	6½
Mexico large - -		0	5	7½
Ditto Small - -		0	5	6¼
Silver in Barrs - - -		0	5	7¼

Annuities

14*l*. per Cent at 22¼ Years Purchase
1704 to 1708 Inclusive 24½ ditto
3¼ per Cent. 1 per Cent. præm.
3 per Cent. 5¼ Disc.

Cochineal 20s od per. lb. *Discount* 00s per Cent.

Lottery 1710.

Prizes for 3 Years from *Michaelmas* last are in course of Payment
Blanks for 3 Years from *Michaelmas* last 1l. 10s *per* Set.

—*Price* of **Stocks**.—	*Wednesday*	*Thursday*	*Friday*
Bank Stock - - - - -	138½ a ¾		138½
East India- - - - - - - -		156	156 a 56¼
South Sea - - - - -	98¾		98¾
Ditto Anuity Old	110½ a 10	110¼	110¼
Ditto——New	110½ a ¾	110¼	110¼
3 *per* Cent. Annuity 1726 - 1731			99¼
Million Bank - - -	113	113	113
Equivalent - - - - - -	112	112	112
R. Aff. 100l paid in L: Aff. 13l paid in	10¼	10¼	10¼
7 per Cent Em. Loan	98	98	98
5 per Cent. Ditto	74¾	74½	75
Bank Circulation	2l 10s od	2l 10s od	2l 10s od
Lottery Tickets	5l 16s od	5l 17s od	6l 00s od

India Transfer Books open the 19th of January
Royal Assurance the 20th of January
South Sea New Annuity the 22d of January, 3 per Cent Annuities the 21st and 22d of January
South Sea Stock the 4th of February
The 5 per Cent Emperor's Loan, sells as above without the six Months Interest of 2 and a quarter per Cent, and 5 per Cent. part of the Principal to be paid of both, are now paying at the Bank
The India Dividend will be paid the 29th of January, South Sea New Annuities the 29th ditto, and the S. Sea Stock the 6th and 7th of February,
Navy and Victualling Bills to the 30th June last are in course of Payment.

—*Interest per Cent*	*Wednesday*	*Thursday*	*Friday*	
3 India Bonds new	79	80	80	Shill: Præm:
4 Salt Tallies	¼ a ½	½ a ½	¼ a ½	

The MARINE LIST.

Gravesend—— Arrived from
30 Dec. Draper, Leach — Dublin
Katherine, Roberts — Figuera
Globe, Harvey — Lisbon
Expedition, Major — Gibralter
1 Industry, Sheppardson — Virginia
Leostoff — arrived from
Swedish Liberty, Vischer — Stockholm
Harwich—— arrived from
Success, Hartley — Gottenburg
Leverpool—— *arrived from*
Dove, Drinkwater — Virginia
Leopard, —— — ditto
Bristol —— *arrived from*
31 Elizabeth, Cheshire — Antigua
Penzance — Arrived from
Anne Sloop, Mitchel — Maderia
Falmouth —— *Arrived* from
27 Cleve, Rice — London
Sailed for
Mary Galley, Cross — Gibralter
Dartmouth—— Arrived from
28 Greenwich, —— — London
Faulker, —— — N.foundland
30 Port Merch. Wallis — Lisbon
Came in for
Mercurius, Waddle — Lisbon
Pool —— Arrived from
27 Watsons Adv. Watson — Lisbon
Rainbow, Skolds — ditto
Patience, Bowles — ditto
29 Betsy, Addis — Carolina
31 Agnes & Mary, Pottle — N.foundland
Wm. & Thomas, Lander — London
Cowes —— Arrived from
29 Brunswick, Payne — Carolina
Carter, Cork — Alderney
Nicholas, Hains — Cherburgh
Came in for
St. Nicholas, Vesseur — Callais
Concordia, Trock — Hamburg
Hellena, Guillaume — Carolina
Dispatch, Wallace — Dublin
Two Maries, Gordon — Southton
Saild for
Neptune, Stevens — Holland
D. of Berwick, Basset — ditto
London, Bourleigh — ditto
Marygold, Joy — ditto
Southampton—— *arrived from*
30 Sarah, Withall — Oporto
Expedition Packet — Guernsey
Sailed for
Martlet, Martin — Amsterdam
Portsmouth —— Arrived from
Came in for
30 Apollo, Brown — Jamaica
Britannia, Tremble — ditto
Enterprize, Wood — Barbadoes
Mahone, Stamper — Gibralter
Gould, Hudson — Carolina
Dover —— *arrived from*
31 Carlisle, Jefferson — Whitehaven

Eagle, Stavely — Biddiford
Mary & Ellen, Rush — Leverpool
——, Slade — ditto
Fidelia, Monkhouse — Dublin
Mary-Ann, Craigh — Limerick
——, Neman — Gottenburg
Nancy, Tracy — Madeira
Downs —— Arrived from
30 K. of Portugal, Hughes — Lisbon
Algarve, Olding — Faro
St. John, Farrel — Antigua
31 Webster, Stevens — Chester
Halsey & Suttle, Salisbury — ditto
1 Marys Reign, Jervoise — Barbadoes
Wm. & Ann, Main — St. Kits
Brittania, Farmer — New-York
Remain for
Two Dutch Ships — EastIndia
A Dutch Ship — Guiney
London, Pipon — Gibralter
Concord, Spilman — Carolina
Ann, Watson — Maryland
Swallow, Hutchinson — Philadelphia
Praleda, Herbert — Cork
Minabilla, Blake — Lisbon
Ann, Ebsworthy — Guiney
Olliver, Pain — Gibralter
Nassau, Spilman — Falmouth
Hannah, Kilpatrick — Portsmouth
Paradox, Righton — St. Kitts

Winds at Deal.

30 SW 31 W 1 NW

Dublin —— *arrived from*
Providence, Steward — London
Edw. & Mary, Littler — ditto
Eagle, — ditto
Cork —— *Arrived from*
15 Martha, Purkess — Southton
Jane & Betty, Jackson — Carolina
William, Higat — Isle of Man
Margaret, Robinson — Dublin
17 Hibernia, Comerford — Bristol
18 St. Louis, Evans — Bourdeaux
19 Richard, Crowley — Dublin
Swift, Denroach — Bristol
20 Success, Allen — Ostend
Mary, Phelan — Waterford
Mary & Betty, M'Goran — Leverpool
Success, Wadmore — Southton
21 Nestor, Moreshin — Havre
Diligence, Milican — Isle of Man
Henry, Richardson — Portsmouth
Margaret, Bryon — Bruges
Two Janes, Portivere — Dublin
3 Brothers, Webb — Bristol
Sailed *bound for*
16 Kath. & Dorothy, Simmonds — Bourd.
18 Brereton, Hammand — Jamaica
19 Lyme Man of War — a Cruize

***Lloyd's List* for 2 January 1740—the earliest known copy**

Roger Lowes: a hot-line to the world's press

Cuthbert Heath

Broker Alana Parry
shows a risk to motor
underwriter Peter
Stilwell

8

All Risks

WHEN Cuthbert Heath wrote the first burglary insurance, he was starting a tradition. The incident took place, as we saw, when a broker was renewing a fire insurance and half-jokingly asked if Heath would also cover the house for burglary since there was a spate of thefts in London at the time.

The idea was completely new, but Heath considered for a moment. 'Why not?' he said, and reached for his pen.

Cuthbert Heath's 'Why not?' has passed into legend. More than that, it has become almost a precept of Lloyd's underwriters to look out for new forms of insurance.

A good example of the 'why not?' spirit was an insurance for the Bank of England, which resulted in the fact that Lloyd's underwriters, emerging from the Room at lunchtime one day in 1967, saw a convoy of armoured cars with a police escort heading up Leadenhall Street towards the Bank of England with £63 million worth of bullion. For the good of their digestions it is perhaps as well that they did not know they had themselves insured it. Each of the five armoured cars was covered at Lloyd's for £15 million, but the market knew nothing about it.

The background to the incident is among the more remarkable examples of Lloyd's sense of trust. Several weeks earlier the Bank of England's broker had approached Robert Gordon, a Lloyd's underwriter specializing in insuring valuables in transit. A large amount of bullion was to be flown from Fort Knox to Mildenhall aerodrome in Suffolk; the Bank wanted to insure it while it was being taken from the airfield to their vaults. There was only one stipulation, which for any ordinary insurance company would have made it unthinkable. Both for political and security reasons, nobody was to know the gold was being moved, or was even present in Britain.

Gordon considered the matter. He knew there was a twelve-month contract in existence for normal sendings and decided it was the sort of situation where Lloyd's both could and ought to help. He mentioned it to one other underwriter, without telling him the subject of the risk or where it was going. The other man agreed that Gordon should accept it on behalf of the underwriters concerned. 'If there had been a loss,' says Gordon, 'I believe the market would have backed my judgment and paid up.' When the Room finally got to hear of what had happened, nobody complained that Gordon's judgment had been wrong.

Since then, machinery has been set up whereby Lloyd's marine market can insure any such exceptional risk without being told the details. The method was used when one of the world's most famous diamonds was taken from New York to London. The slip contained a clause saying simply that all security should be agreed by the leading underwriter; other underwriters, though they had a huge risk on it, do not know to this day how the diamond travelled.

Gordon, recently retired from the market, is one of the characters who make Lloyd's. Noted for his deadpan wit and the red rose he always wore in his buttonhole, he wrote art-treasures as well as bullion and marine risks. Through him, the marine market set up its own security department, run by an ex-Scotland Yard man, to supervise the safety of works of art in transit. When one famous work, Goya's portrait of the Duke of Wellington, had to be taken from a gallery to the airport, the former Scotland Yard man carried it down Bond Street, wrapped merely in a piece of sacking. 'It seemed,' Gordon recalls, 'the best way to attract least attention.'

Another time Gordon's caution not only saved himself and other underwriters a lot of money; it possibly saved one of the world's masterpieces from destruction. The incident happened when the Leonardo da Vinci cartoon was exhibited at Burlington House as part of the campaign to raise £800,000 to keep it in the country. 'One day the gallery got a letter from a crank,' says Gordon, 'saying he was going to damage it because he thought the money could be better spent. Because of the warning, we asked the gallery if they'd cover it with perspex just in case. They didn't like the idea but agreed. A few weeks later someone threw a bottle of ink at it. The claim was seventeen quid, instead of £800,000.'

Julian Radcliffe of the brokers Hogg Robinson is also a 'why not?' man. Though he has not yet achieved the fame of Cuthbert Heath, he has, at the age of thirty-eight, made some remarkable innovations in the market. Crackling with energy and intelligence, he looks more like an academic high-flyer than a broker. What you would certainly not suspect is that he has linked Lloyd's to the cloak-and-dagger world of terrorists and kidnaps.

When he came down from Oxford in 1970, Radcliffe started work at Sir Peter Green's box. While still a scratch-boy—the jargon name for the junior who is regarded as the lowest form of underwriting life—Radcliffe quickly conceived some ideas of his own about the market. This was the period of massive construction in the Middle East, and also the rise of potentially threatening regimes in such places as Libya and Uganda. Radcliffe's idea was that Lloyd's should be able to provide cover for exporters who were sending valuable plant to countries where there was a considerable risk that it might be lost through, for example, local wars or political expropriation. In the past, there had been various government schemes through which exporters could cover themselves against such risks. But what Radcliffe planned was the creation of a new commercial market.

In 1971 he put down his ideas about what he called political risks on paper. Sir Peter Green and another leading underwriter, Stephen Merrett, were both interested, but thought it would be necessary to use a specialist broker who would bring in enough clients to create a spread of business. The result was that Radcliffe was seconded to Hogg Robinson to set up the broking end in the form of a new company called Investment Insurance International. By the end of the first year, it was generating enough business to convince the underwriters that political risks could become a profitable market. Even so, the early years brought some dodgy times for the underwriters. One of the first risks the company took on was the insurance of the overseas assets of one major electronics group, which included a plant in Portugal. During the revolution there, the plant was taken over, semi-nationalized, but then released. 'It never became a claim but it was a near-run thing,' says Radcliffe. 'We had an even narrower miss when we nearly insured an African trading company which, within three weeks of our quoting to them, were nationalized in Uganda with the loss of several million.'

Meanwhile Radcliffe was already beginning to see the importance of what is now recognized in the market as his trademark: the creation of a back-up scheme which would help to limit losses. 'Any type of insurance starts with the policy,' he says, 'But subsequently the back-up service becomes as important as the policy itself. In fire insurance, for example, the policy-holder spends more money on sprinklers to prevent fire, than on the actual insurance. On political risks, we created additional services whose aim was to reduce the risks by vetting contracts, controlling investment, and recovering debts wherever possible.'

Meanwhile Radcliffe was spending a lot of time going round talking to various international corporations, and during his talks with them he was gradually becoming aware of a new need. A number of his clients had told him they were concerned about the safety of their personnel. By then there had been a few kidnappings in Latin America, and some of the companies were beginning to think about taking out insurance. Radcliffe, who had studied terrorism in Beirut in 1970 while on a travel scholarship from Oxford, produced a paper outlining the possibilities and problems.

The idea of kidnap insurance was, he knew, controversial. If the would-be kidnappers knew that a potential victim was insured, would it encourage them to go ahead in the knowledge that the ransom would be forthcoming from insurers? What he also knew was that every new form of insurance has always raised comparable doubts. It was said of fire insurance, in its early days, that it would encourage arson.

In 1974, a relatively small amount of kidnap and ransom insurance was being written at Lloyd's, who insisted that it must be virtually impossible for a kidnap gang to know if their victim was insured. The name of the person insured should be coded, and be known only to the underwriter and the broker. Most kidnap business was led by one specialist syndicate, that of Cassidy, Davies. Radcliffe put up the idea to Anthony Cassidy, the leading underwriter, that the chances of a loss could be reduced by teaching a potential victim to take precautions. One example that might be followed, he thought, was that of the SAS who had instructed ambassadors and foreign embassy staff on such principles as disruption of their routines. Additionally, Radcliffe thought, the insurance market might go further. There could be ways in which staff could be provided who could actually help during negotiations with the kidnappers, by checking events and ensuring that the victim's family did not panic or pay up too quickly. In effect, it was an extension of Radcliffe's guiding principle of back-up—the idea that, along with the policy, the market itself should provide some form of loss-prevention. By the end of 1974 he had set up, within Hogg Robinson, a new company called Control Risks—recruited largely from former SAS officers.

In 1974, even the kidnap and ransom underwriters were sceptical about how far Radcliffe's idea would work out. 'Before Control Risks began,' he recalls, 'the underwriters were advising the use of local lawyers to conduct negotiations over ransoms, but there was no attempt to monitor the position. We proposed to them that we could take the first case for no fee, just our man's expenses. As it happened, it was a case in Italy, and at first the underwriters were unwilling to pay for our man to stay more than a few days. What then happened proved our point. As long as he was there he kept the situation stable. But when he left, the family began to panic and to raise their offer. So it became apparent that we had to have someone there all the time, and gradually the underwriters started to accept this.'

Soon Control Risks was gaining enough of a reputation for skill in handling kidnaps that local police forces began to accept the idea of liaising with them. Control Risks men do not actually meet the kidnappers. Negotiations on the phone are usually done by a friend of the family, if possible a lawyer. 'The Control Risks man will school him and organize a strategy,' Radcliffe says. 'He can say to the family, look we've been through all this before, you've just got to be very patient.'

Today Control Risks staff have become so internationally regarded as experts in their field that they are asked to train many police forces in anti-kidnap methods. Though the Cassidy syndicate does not insist that clients commission Control Risks' services, it will rebate up to ten per cent of an assured's first premium if he consults them and uses their precautionary measures. 'If Control Risks hadn't existed, people would have paid more money more easily and the terrorists would have been better funded,' Radcliffe sums up.

Radcliffe seems unlikely to be content with his achievements so far. Following his guiding rule that it is the back-up service that is all-important, he is now moving into areas where the interests of the insurance market coincide with those of social usefulness. In the area of what Lloyd's calls fine arts insurance, for instance, he is currently developing the idea of a registry of stolen works of art whose existence would inform dealers—rather like a bank's list of stopped cheques—that they were stolen.

But Radcliffe's most startling and creative idea—it is already under close consideration by Lloyd's and some company insurers—is for a scheme for a swifter and more efficient settlement of serious bodily injury claims. 'At the moment,' he says, 'in the case of a road accident, even if it is clear that the driver was at fault, all parties stand miles apart. Insurers will not admit liability until the passenger comes at them, and the lawyers on both sides will argue for up to three years. Eventually there will be a settlement, probably on the doorstep of the court, for a lump sum which the victim may then squander.'

'The new idea is that the initial emphasis should be on rehabilitation. As soon as someone has been injured, our expert loss management team will see his solicitor, and try to put together some suitable package for returning him to work. For example, they would be able to suggest how a former house-painter might receive re-training as a commercial artist. Instead of lying waiting for the day when he gets a million pounds, he will be helped at once to begin a new life. In one sense this is a very similar idea to Control Risks—but designed for an entirely different purpose.'

The sense of 'why not?' can relate not only to an individual risk like the Bank of England's bullion. Sometimes it results in the creation of a whole new market, as it did with offshore oil.

The modern offshore market—where over $1 billion insurance for a production platform can be placed with the agreement of six underwriters in a single morning—is one area where Lloyd's supremacy is undisputed. It also stems from something which has always been strong at Lloyd's—a feeling that, as a service industry, insurance should be there to help commerce meet its challenges and new needs.

Though values have increased many times over, the offshore market today differs little in essentials from that which began in 1958, when a group of marine underwriters evolved what is known as the London drilling rig memorandum. This was the agreement under which they wrote business for US coverholders, or surplus line brokers who were the channel to London for US drilling contractors then preparing to range the oceans in quest of offshore oil and gas.

But even for the world's most experienced marine market, the new type of business was a major challenge. On the one hand, it represented a new premium source, in an area where no-one was competing. On the other hand Lloyd's had to grapple with the problems of insuring new, hugely expensive, often unproven structures. One underwriter observed: 'We had to come to terms with a kind of vessel that wasn't even going to be manned by sailors.'

At first the new business seemed to do moderately well. Then came disaster. First Hurricane Betsy brought severe losses in 1965, and in the next nine months, a series of separate losses in places ranging from the Gulf of Mexico to Australia brought in huge claims. Till then,

Lloyd's—the leading underwriters were the Janson Green and Chester syndicates—had been writing rig risks at three per cent. Now the question was whether they could find a rate that would enable the market to continue. 'Probably the true rate should have been fifteen per cent,' recalls Henry Chester. 'But we had to find some sort of compromise. The Rig Committee was determined to maintain Lloyd's reputation for responding to the needs of a new industry.'

What happened next was something that has never happened before or since: the offshore underwriters virtually went on strike. They declared a three week moratorium on all offshore business, while a deal was worked out with the brokers. Towards the end of the three weeks the Rig Committee came up with a rate of ten per cent. The brokers demurred. Could the underwriters make a small reduction? The market came back with 9.75 per cent. The brokers agreed, and from 24 June 1966 the London offshore market was in business.

The other important outcome of the talks was that it laid down the principles on which, over the last twenty years, offshore risks have been placed and written in the market. 'The underwriters at that time were steadfast in their view that the new class of business could only be written on a uniform basis,' says Jonathan Gilbert of Sedgwick, who had led the brokers. The result was that all offshore risks became channelled through the single contract called the London Drilling Master Slip. Evolved from the earlier London drilling rig memorandum, it is what Lloyd's calls an 'open slip', meaning that it is available to several brokers and placed with a select number of leading underwriters who are empowered by others on the slip to make decisions. Though Sedgwick continues to have the largest share, any broker may use the market slip if he can show a volume of business large enough to justify his presence on what is still the largest single contract of its kind in world insurance markets.

'Journalists', observed Peter Stilwell, the motor underwriter, 'are a bad lot.'

It was not, he assured me, anything personal. It was just that journalists are among the professions that his syndicate would not insure without further information on their record as drivers. My fellow-undesirables, it seemed, included actors, sportsmen, convicted drivers, probation officers, bookmakers and people who run casinos.

Weren't probation officers rather responsible citizens? Again, there was nothing personal, said Peter Stilwell. 'But not long ago we had a probation officer who was taking one of his clients somewhere in his car, and the client clonked him on the head. That's something we look out for.'

About one person in five in Britain insures his car with one or other of the forty syndicates that make up Lloyd's motor market. It is a market that differs from others in that the syndicates are named, on the assumption that people like to identify their policy with something that sounds like a company, not just someone's surname. Much of the business actually written in the Room relates to fleets of company cars—some go up to premium values in the region of £2m—while most individual policies are handled in the underwriter's office.

Peter Stilwell's HGP syndicate is one of the top three, writing £27m of the market's total premium of around £500m. Recently the syndicate has developed a considerable market in insuring large blocks of company cars. 'We said to some of the leading brokers,' Peter Stilwell says, 'that they must have a lot of big commercial clients. Why not get them to bring their employees' motor business to the market?' The result has been what is called the payroll deduction scheme, where staffs of large companies can get a discount on car insurance premiums, with premiums deducted from their pay-cheques. The syndicate is also notable as having been the first to introduce computers and VDUs into Lloyd's. Computerized statistics, said Peter Stilwell, had helped them to spot that a certain make of vehicle had been costing the syndicate a lot in fire-claims. They had initiated an investigation, and found a fault with the fuel-feeder clip. The result had been a new design, safer motoring, with a reduction in the market's losses.

Apart from the unfortunate nature of my trade, I asked, what other factors would affect my getting an insurance?

'It depends what sort of car you want to drive.' He showed me his manual which grades various makes. Types of cars are classified by numbers, ranging from Fiestas and Minis which are in group one, to Lotuses and Ferraris which go up to seventeen. If I had a Porsche and planned to take it overseas, that would add a lot more. 'The big German cars are noted for their disappearing act when they get to Italy,' said Peter, looking sombre.

Another formula divides the country into areas for rates. In principle, country areas are charged at lower rates than metropolitan districts like Manchester or London. One day, he had been host to a party from Hendon Police College in the Room. One of them had described how he'd been doing some underwater work in an Essex gravel-pit, looking for a body. 'He said he hadn't found any bodies, but there were an awful lot of cars down there. That's what you've got to reckon on, around the cities.' Even when you get away from the metropolitan areas, rates vary a good deal. Dorset is one of the cheapest, but your insurance will cost more if you get near to Bournemouth. If you live in Lancashire south of the River Ribble you pay rather more than if you live north of Morecambe Bay.

We went over to the HGP box, where an older broker and a young one were already waiting.

'I've got a few things for you. Spreading from good to bad.' The younger broker opened up his slipcase.

'The bad news is he's here at all.' Peter had by now assumed the dry, judicious, deadpan look that is part of the underwriter's stock-in-trade, along with his pen and blotting-paper.

The broker produced various papers from his case. There was an additional premium to be paid for a client who had had a drinking conviction, some green cards to be checked, while the Croydon branch of a big Japanese company wanted some premium returned because they had reduced their car-fleet.

'Not my favourite pastime, returning premium.' All the same, Peter scribbled an initial.

The next risk was for another company fleet, which had been insured with the syndicate some while back. It was on offer at the moment because it had come back to the market from one of the company insurers. It was a big fleet, the broker said, and the company were looking for a low premium in return for some rather large excesses.

Peter studied the slip. It listed what looked to be a very high incidence of claims over the last five years. 'I don't think,' he said courteously, 'I want to get into a new risk at this sort of premium.'

The broker said hopefully that it was going to take a lot of private cars to make that sort of money, but by now Peter had got the slightly brooding look of an underwriter sensing trouble. He scrawled a ring round the accident figures on the claims form. 'It's also going to take up a lot of people's time covering all those claims. No thanks, I don't think I like it.'

By now it was the older broker's turn and he moved in with some cheerful banter about what stupendous rates the underwriters were charging. His business was a slightly tricky claim—the assured was a company fleet, based somewhere in mid-Glamorgan. One of the firm's employees had had his car stolen, and it had then been damaged while the thief was driving. What rather spoilt things, the car-owner admitted, was that he had left it unlocked in his drive, with the key in the ignition.

Peter flicked through the papers on the file. The estimate for repairs was for £425 plus the parts. The syndicate had replied to that with a rather non-committal letter saying they didn't see that they could be held responsible since the car had not been locked. The assured's response had been an apologetic letter saying that he had had to move his girlfriend's car to make room for his own car on the drive, and he was sorry he'd then forgotten to go back and lock his own car.

The broker looked up, a touch anxiously, as Peter closed his file. 'Do you think you can do something for him, sir?'

Peter had assumed his deadpan look. I felt I was getting to know how underwriters ticked by now. If I'd had to guess what he was going to do about the claim, I'd have said he was going to reject it.

Instead he scrawled a quick initial. 'We'll pay that claim. After all, we're getting a premium of £100,000 on the fleet. And then, mid-Glamorgan isn't central London.'

The broker beamed with evident relief. 'That's very nice of you, sir. I really appreciate that.'

'All part of the service. And the flexibility of Lloyd's.'

They both smiled, as Lloyd's people do when the market suddenly shows that it is human.

It would clearly be too time-consuming if every individual car policy had to be taken to an underwriter by a broker. To find out how ordinary policies are placed, I went to see Terry Wellard, who is a leading motor broker.

He turned out to be a friendly, laid-back man in his middle forties, with a typical broker's conversational panache. We sat down in his office not far from Old Street station—motor brokers tend to have slightly more workaday surroundings than the broker barons—which contained photos of his two racehorses winning. To put me in the picture about what is known as the direct motor scheme, he said, we had better go back to the beginning. His firm, Edgar Hamilton, is a wholesale broker. This means that eighty per cent of its business consists of placing risks at Lloyd's which have originated from High Street brokers in the suburbs or provinces. Among other things, he said, Edgar Hamilton might help a provincial broker to place a Lloyd's policy for a local parachute club, or for promoters of a golf club tournament who wanted to cover themselves against the chance of a lot of people getting a hole-in-one cash prize. The business also included household insurance but the main area was motor business.

'Till the 1960s,' Terry Wellard said, 'motor insurance was broked at Lloyd's in the conventional sense of the broker going to the box. But even by then it was becoming uneconomic as a way of handling private motor business. The other point was a lot of the business was coming from the High Street brokers. The big step came when the Committee of Lloyd's decided that the market could accept these risks—so long as they were placed under the guarantee of a Lloyd's broker like ourselves, who would guarantee the premium to the underwriter.'

So what happened, I asked, if a motorist wanted to take out a Lloyd's policy from his local broker in Manchester or Bolton?

'All right, let's say Fred Smith of Bolton wants car insurance. He goes to his local broker and asks for a quotation. The broker can quote a price, based on the guidelines you heard about from Peter Stilwell. Assuming the quotation is acceptable, he fills in a proposal form. The broker has authority to effect cover for him immediately, so Fred Smith walks out of the Bolton office covered by Lloyd's underwriters.

'Over the next few days, the broker will forward a copy of the cover note and the proposal form direct to the Lloyd's underwriter's office. When the underwriter receives this, he sends the policy document and certificate, with a debit note, to the Bolton broker. At the end of each month's transactions, the underwriter sends out a statement asking for payment—with a copy to, for example, ourselves, as the guaranteeing broker.

'Meanwhile the broker in Bolton has collected the premium from Fred Smith. After he's deducted his own commission, he pays the premium to the guaranteeing broker, who then takes his commission and pays the underwriter.

'The underwriter can sleep at night because, even if anything goes wrong with the Bolton broker, he knows he'll get his money from the guaranteeing broker.'

The direct dealing system, continued Terry Wellard, was the first-ever move by Lloyd's towards the High Street. But Lloyd's would not be Lloyd's unless there were some out-of-the-way risks alongside the bread-and-butter ones. Edgar Hamilton have two motor brokers who spend all their time in the Room, placing not only the company cars I had seen at Peter Stilwell's box, but special policies on vintage cars, accident-prone motorists or fleets of thirty-two trucks, and special

risks of that sort. I asked what the most expensive private motor policy
would be. Terry Wellard thought for a bit and then said it would be for
a twenty-year-old pop star who drove a Porsche and lived in Hampstead. What, I asked, would be the premium for that? He scratched his
head and finally rang one of his underwriting friends who made a
shuddering sound clearly audible on the telephone across the room,
and said you'd got to be talking about £5,000 worth of premium.

We moved on to the subject of container trucks, where he told me
the equipment will often be more expensive than the vehicle itself. For
example, the damage caused by even a minor bump to the equipment
of a refrigerated truck could be colossal. 'Or take concrete-mixer lor-
ries. If one of them has an accident, it has to be dealt with literally in
minutes, because if the concrete goes solid it's a write-off. Then you
get a lorry going to Saudi Arabia across the middle of the desert. If it's
involved in a minor accident, the driver has to shunt it to the roadside.
Before you know where you are it'll either be vandalized or have sunk
into the sand—and your minor bump's become a total loss. People
think our business is just about one bump against another. There's a
lot more than that to motor business.'

If you happen to spot an underwriter deep in the pages of *The Sporting
Life* at his box, it is unlikely he will be studying form for his own
amusement. He is likely to be the specialist livestock underwriter
Terry Hall, who in his time has insured everything in the four-footed,
not to say zoological line, from Derby winners to the Loch Ness Monster, as well as the odd skating elephant or boxing kangaroo.

A number of marine syndicates write some livestock insurance, but
Terry Hall, a big, relaxed man with the look of a countryman himself,
is the acknowledged expert.

In the mercantile world of Lloyd's the work of the livestock underwriter may seem to strike a pastoral note, but it is by no means always
peaceful. Nowadays when so many animals are being carried around
the world, racehorses have to be insured against the harrowing possibility of their going berserk in aircraft. One headline story that came
close to Terry Hall's box was that of Shergar, the great Irish racehorse
that vanished after being kidnapped. It had been, he explained, a complex matter for Shergar's insurers. The horse had been owned by a
syndicate, some of whose members had taken out insurance that
covered theft, while others hadn't. A further complication had been
that in law, theft meant 'with intent to permanently deprive' which was

a different matter from extortion. In the end, the underwriters had decided that the people who had taken out theft insurance had believed themselves to be covered to the best possible extent, so they had made an ex-gratia payment which had cost the market £7m.

Chatting with Terry Hall and his deputy John Bovington makes you feel as if you were at Newmarket Heath instead of Lloyd's of London. In their office basement, they said, they kept all the old formbooks. If you wanted to check on any horse over the last thirty years, they could look it up there. 'I've still got the slip,' Terry reminisced, 'for My Babu that won the 2,000 Guineas in 1948. Owned by the Maharanee of Baroda. The lead-line on it was £2,000. Nowadays we write lead-lines of half a million.'

John Bovington told me about a newly-devised policy to cover someone selling a yearling at the sales against the possibility of its failing a pre-sale wind-examination. 'If it makes a whistling and roaring noise like a car with carburettor trouble, it won't be allowed anywhere near the sale-ring, and the chances are remote that it would ever be sold as a potential racehorse.'

Terry Hall added that they didn't only insure horses that were alive and kicking. 'We insure them before they're born, against the risk of being aborted or born dead. It could cost someone up to £1m to get his mare served by a horse like Northern Dancer. If the mare produces a foal it might be worth up to £5m. But if the service doesn't take, the owner's going to need insurance.'

We moved on to discussing covering mares, not in the insurance sense, and then to stallion infertility insurance. This would be important to you, Terry said, if you were fortunate enough to be the owner of next year's Derby winner or a horse like Shareef Dancer, which has been insured for as much as $40m. 'You'd be thinking about the time when you're going to realize your assets by putting him to stud. It's a bit like selling futures.' One famous horse, Secretariat, had been covered for $10m against failing a fertility test. 'When the horse did fail the test we offered to pay, provided we could keep the horse as salvage. This didn't go down very well with the assured, so we said that if sixty per cent of his first batch of mares failed to conceive, we'd pay. However, in the end he had a ninety-eight per cent success-rate.'

Afterwards I went back with them to their box, where I heard about some of the other livestock. What with policies on prize bulldogs, pumas and guppy fish, it was a bit like an insurance man's Noah's Ark.

The first broker to come up said he had now got the answer to a query they had had the previous day, about a bird called a trumpeter.

'That's right. We thought it was a sort of swan, didn't we?'

'Apparently it's more like a small crane.'

Terry Hall scribbled a note on a bit of paper, initialled the slip, and looked at a sheet of telex. It was from a client who wanted to renew the insurance on a lot of cattle and horses somewhere in Andalusia, but apparently thought the rate should be cut.

'He won't learn, will he.' Terry studied the telex sadly. 'I like José, but there's nothing doing.'

Another broker moved to the top of the queue—he wanted to know how much it would cost to include the berserk clause on a racehorse travelling by air.

'Point one two five per cent.'

The broker asked if you spelt berserk with a 'z', and Terry Hall said no, with an 's'. 'It's an old Norse word. From when the Vikings used to fight each other. They went all bleary-eyed and frothing.'

'Sounds like a Lloyd's broker,' said the broker, and moved off.

The next man had a claim on some ostriches that had been taken by air from South Africa to the United States. It seemed two had broken their legs in transit, and had to be destroyed. Terry Hall said on this one he honestly thought they had a case against the shipper.

'It says here that the shipper is not responsible for death due to natural causes. That suggests that he is responsible if it's not a natural cause.'

They both went into a long discussion about what a natural cause was, then decided they'd go away and think about it. Afterwards I asked Terry what would happen, and he said that in livestock insurance a dead animal was really nine-tenths of a claim. 'In a case like this, we'll honour the claim. Then we'll try to get something back from the shipper later.'

I asked him what had been his most outlandish risk, and he said he supposed it had been when a whisky firm had offered a million-pound prize to anyone who could actually produce the Loch Ness Monster. 'After they'd offered the prize, they suddenly got cold feet. It occurred to them that somebody might actually claim it. We took two-and-a-half thousand premium off them, and I warranted that the monster had to be caught by fair angling, which means by rod and line. It also had to be twenty feet long, and approved by the Natural History Museum.

The last bit we put in as a joke—we said it had to be produced live, and handed over to the underwriters as salvage.'

There was a footnote to the Loch Ness Monster story. Some Aberdeen fishermen caught a sea-elephant, which was dead when they hauled it aboard their trawler. They often went through the Caledonian Canal to fish off the west coast, and for a joke they disguised the sea-elephant by cutting off its whiskers, then dropped it off in Loch Ness. A few days later someone fishing in the loch had foulhooked it, and it had been landed. The news of the discovery had been on the radio one Saturday lunchtime when Terry was digging in his garden. 'I was out there digging when my wife came out to tell me they thought they'd caught the Loch Ness Monster. I called out 'How long was it?' and she called back that it had been seventeen feet. So I went on digging. As long as it was under twenty feet, we were all right.'

9

'Touching the Adventures and Perils . . .'

Touching the Adventures and Perils which we the Assurers are contented to bear and do take upon us in this Voyage, they are, of the Seas, Men-of-War, Fire, Enemies, Pirates, Rovers, Thieves, Jettisons, Letters of Mart and Countermart, Surprisals, Takings at Sea, Arrests, Restraints and Detainments of all Kings, Princes and People, of what Nation, Condition or Quality soever, Barratry of the Master and Mariners and of all other Perils, Losses and Misfortunes . . .

SUCH, in the words of Lloyd's Marine Insurance Policy of 1779, were the Adventures and Perils—the possible disasters which a ship-owner could claim for.

Today, nearly two hundred years later, the range of possibilities is somewhat greater. It may not include Barratry of the Master, Letters of Mart or Pirates. On the other hand the twentieth century can all too easily produce its own equivalents, from hijacking to war risks and earthquakes to pollution.

In the summer of 1984, five major air disasters in three months cost Lloyd's aviation underwriters $183m. The previous year, marine underwriters had paid out $43m on a single vessel. Such huge sums may be the exception, but even in an ordinary year, just on £6 billion worth of claims are made on Lloyd's underwriters.

The story of how they are assessed, worked out and paid, is the story of Lloyd's Claims Office.

'Mind you don't shift that manhole. There's still gas in her holds.'

From somewhere down the Rhine waterway came the wailing scraping sound of a dredger; in the great Verolme shipyard a sparkle of blue acetylene flared and died against the winter sky. Mr Harry Thurston, the Ship Surveyor at Rotterdam, adjusted his tin hat, then led the way into the burnt-out afterhouse. It was a bit like going into a stalactite cave, eerie, dark, with bits of twisted metal hanging from the ceiling.

'That was the electric control for pumping the oil.' Mr Thurston flicked on his torch and we peered into a blackened room that led from the deckhouse. You could just see the outline of what had been the control panel, swollen and shapeless like a slab of stone.

We came out from the afterhouse to the deck—everywhere there was a reddish soil-like substance where the bitumen surface had melted. The afterhouse windows had caved in so it had the look of a ruined castle. Halfway along the deck a couple of men were hauling up cans of sludge on a sort of pulley.

Of all the Perils and Adventures listed in the Lloyd's policy of 1779 there is still one that is a terrifying word to any seaman, and that is fire. It was fire which had struck this ship, the *Trilantic*. She had been bound for Leixoes in Portugal from the Persian Gulf with a load of crude oil six months before when fire had broken out in her engine room. One man had been killed, the duty engineer, who had stayed in the engine room to try to turn off the oil valves. The rest of the crew had been picked up by a Russian tanker, and the still-smouldering *Trilantic* towed to Gibraltar. From there she had been brought to Rotterdam for her oil to be discharged. Now the long and complicated task of surveying her was beginning.

As we picked our way gingerly down the twisted companion-ways, Mr Thurston explained that he was not strictly speaking employed by Lloyd's—the Salvage Association, which he represents in Rotterdam, is an organization looking after the interests of all London underwriters. In this case the ship had been insured at Lloyd's. If she was eventually written off as a total loss, the claim would be in the region of $10 million.

'Do you think she will be a total loss?' Looking down the great length of deck it seemed likely. Of all inanimate objects few things are sadder than a ship that has been swept by fire.

'It's a question of what the owner decides.' Mr Thurston explained that there had already been long discussions with the owner—even the actual decision to bring the *Trilantic* to Rotterdam had been worked out in consultation between him and the Salvage Association. The reason for this was that the *Trilantic* was not a conventional tanker but what was called an OBO.

'It isn't a kind of musical instrument,' Mr Thurston comes from Hartlepool; after twenty-one years abroad he still has a hint of the bent vowels of the north-east. 'It stands for an Oil Bulk Ore carrier. The point is that her holds are specially constructed.' Because of this, he explained, there had been a considerable problem about discharging her cargo of 68,000 tons of crude oil. If it hadn't been done in exactly the right way, she could have keeled over while being emptied in the dry dock. Eventually it had been decided that only the port of Rotterdam had the necessary facilities.

Now that the oil had been safely discharged, the next thing would be to see how badly she was damaged—the owners' fear, Mr Thurston said, was that her whole stern quarter might have been pushed out of alignment. 'In that case he might have to rebuild the whole stern and afterhouse, which would cost more than she's insured for.' A lot of tests had been carried out, he said, in dry-dock—now she was afloat again and there would be more tests. One way and another it looked like being a fairly complicated claim, but so were most of the claims that came his way as a Ship Surveyor. In his office at Schiedam he had four surveyors working under him, and they dealt with everything from colliding coasters to recovering cargoes from ships that had been stranded.

If the Salvage Association was instructed by Lloyd's, I asked, wasn't any survey bound to be biased in favour of the underwriter and against the owner? Mr Thurston stressed very strongly that it wasn't—the Latin motto of the Association, he said, meant 'Seek the Truth', and they meant it. In the twenty years he had been with the Salvage Association he had always seen his job as to make sure that all claims were settled fairly and reasonably, and he couldn't remember one that wasn't.

All his life, Mr Thurston said, he had had a twin passion for ships and football. Before working for the Salvage Association he had been a ship's engineer with the Blue Funnel Line, then with smaller tramp steamers operating from his home town. 'I gravitated back to my original level,' he said, with a grin, 'West Hartlepool.' Since joining the Salvage Association he had worked in Cardiff, Antwerp, Hamburg and Rotterdam, where for the last five years he had run a football club called the Pirates made up of a mixture of Dutch, English and Belgians. All the same, the team he really supported was from just about the only place he had never worked in—Manchester United.

Meanwhile, he suggested that if I'd like to put on my tin hat again we might go down and have a look at the engine room. There wasn't much to see, but a few technicians were down there working on the engine alignment. We went down a couple more companionways, then along a stretch of metal deck which had been bent and buckled so there was water lying in deep puddles. Then we were in the dark again. When we emerged it was into a huge area like a great cave.

'This was the engine room.' Mr Thurston looked round. There were a few naked bulbs but the light only made it seem more garish. Everywhere there was blackened metal and blistered bulkheads. In the centre were the seven cylinders of what had been the ship's main engine.

'The water came right up to the height of those cylinders.' Mr Thurston shone his torch towards them, and I peered down. They must have been forty feet up.

We edged slowly down a ripped-up platform, then down a ladder. With bits of metal hanging over us at head height, I could see the point of the tin hats.

'Like Dante's *Inferno* the day after.' Mr Thurston shone his torch into a small, blackened control room—it was here, he said, that the duty engineer had died in the fire. 'This is where it started. Like the pillar of flame in the Bible. It must have just gone through the deck-house in minutes.'

He flicked off the torch, and we made our way slowly back along the blackened companionways. After the grimness of the burnt-out engine room, even the cold wind on deck was a relief. In the distance the coasters slid past the entrance of the Rhine waterway—the deceptive calmness, it occurred to me, of a world of ships.

'*Touching the Perils which are of the Seas, Men-of-War, Fire* . . . '

After two hundred years, they seemed as real as ever.

Insurers, like newspapermen, thrive on disaster. If no ship ever sank, nobody would insure them. From the kind of multi-million dollar risks that Lloyd's writes, down to your and my burglary insurance, claims are what it is all about. Whether a claim is paid quickly or not is the yardstick by which most people judge insurers.

But claims are not always cut-and-dried, as I learnt when I called on Mr Len Watson, General Manager of Lloyd's Underwriters Claims and Recoveries Office, known as LUCRO. Mr Watson's department deals with most claims on marine underwriters' accounts, and his ninth-floor office window, suitably for a marine man, looks over Seething Lane, where Samuel Pepys had his office as Secretary of the Navy.

Mr Watson has been in Claims for thirty-eight years and he reckons, modestly and happily, that he has probably the most interesting job in Lloyd's. 'No two days are ever the same and no two claims are ever the same,' he says. 'In the vast majority of cases, the claim is settled in full and we like to believe that most settlements are very speedy. A claim that requires no query at all should be settled in a week, or not much longer. Of course, there are a lot of claims that do need looking into. But primarily our job is to pay claims, not reject them.'

A typical example of the kind of problem that the market was faced with nowadays, he said, was when it was unclear whether a claim should be paid under the normal casualty cover or as a war risk. A recent example had been that of the Air India jet which had crashed in 1984, killing over 300 people. It had never been finally established whether the loss was due to a terrorist bomb or an aircraft fault. But both sets of underwriters had been keen that payment to Air India should be as prompt as possible, and as an interim compromise, both the all-risks and war risk underwriters had paid half.

In the marine market, the longest-running claims problem in recent years has been that of the seventy ships trapped, since the beginning of the Iran–Iraq war, in the Shatt-el-Arab waterway on the Iraqi border. 'The unusual situation here,' Len Watson told me, 'is that we have paid out for total losses on all seventy ships—though at the time of settlement most of them were sitting there undamaged. They were insured against war perils, and in some cases against what we call "blocking and trapping" which is effectively what happened to them.'

From the underwriters' point of view, the whole episode had meant a severe loss, amounting to just on $350m for the seventy vessels. And to make matters worse, there seemed no possibility of getting anything back. The 'Recoveries' part of LUCRO's name is meaningful for underwriters. In insurance terms a recovery is whatever an underwriter manages to recoup, often in the form of a salvaged cargo, when he has paid a big claim. In an earlier and not dissimilar incident in the 1960s, when fifteen ships had been trapped in the Suez Canal during the Six-Day War, underwriters had gained something to set against their losses because the value of some of the ships' metal cargoes had gone up dramatically during the eight years they had been trapped in the Canal.

But on the Shatt-el-Arab ships, Len Watson doubted that much would come back in the form of recoveries or salvage. 'One of the differences compared to Suez was that the Shatt-el-Arab ships all had empty holds. As to the question of recovering their hulls, the point is that the bar at the mouth of the Shatt-el-Arab silts up very fast. Even after two years, to have desilted it would have cost several million dollars. So that even if it were possible to get the ships out, it wouldn't be worth the expense of taking most of them to the nearest scrapyard at Karachi.'

The claims world has altered dramatically over the last twenty-five years. One area where values have soared is the North Sea, where it is common for a drilling-rig's insured value to reach £100m. The relatively new area of political risks has brought some mammoth claims, while more striking still is the area of pollution risks, of which Lloyd's marine underwriters had their first sharp experience in 1967, when oil from the stricken *Torrey Canyon* flooded British and French beaches. Lloyd's marine market was not only liable for the loss of the ship—but her owners were asked by the British and French governments to pay compensation in the region of what was then the vast sum of £6m. This was not only to cover such things as the use of the RAF and the clearing of oil from the beaches. Compensation, the governments said, had to be made to hotel-keepers, fishermen and people who hired boats out. In the end, the underwriters settled for £3m. 'I remember my predecessor, Dick Rutherford, making a good point,' Watson recalls. 'He said how do you assess the loss of revenue to an ice-cream man when his loss might have been due to the fact that it was a bad summer?'

Because many marine underwriters cover land risks as well, LUCRO had been involved in some startling US claims on environment pollution where claims can run into billions. 'You get the impression that the United States is splattered with waste-dumps which people have created without thinking too much about the future,' says Watson. Of 26,000 hazardous waste sites identified to date, he mentioned one in New York State. Ironically known as Love Canal, it had been capped off with clay in the early 1950s. The area had then been sold off and a school and housing estate built on it. But subsequent excavations had breached the clay, and soon the residents were complaining of serious health disorders. In 1978 Love Canal had been declared a disaster area. Nobody knows yet what the underwriters eventual bill might be, but the cost of remedial action for this and three other nearby sites has been assessed at over $400m.

Lloyd's biggest-ever single marine claim arose in 1979 when the Ogden Corporation's shipyard at Avondale, New Orleans, began trials of three newly-built gas-carriers which used a new form of insulation. During the trials, serious faults were found in the process, which meant that the ships were virtually useless for the purpose they had been built for. After long negotiations, the claim was eventually settled for $300m.

Of all the perils and adventures, the one most intriguing to the layman is the type of loss caused by marine fraud. The practice of scuttling—or as Lloyd's men discreetly put it 'throwing away' a ship for the insurance money—is as old as insurance itself. Over the last twenty years, numerous new types of maritime fraud have been devised to cheat shippers, cargo-owners, governments—and, as a consequence, insurers. Banks have been persuaded to advance huge sums on the strength of bills of lading which listed non-existent cargoes. Cargoes, already paid for by one shipper, have been sold in other ports to the highest bidder. Scuttling, the oldest form of marine fraud, has increased partly, Mr Watson thinks, because of world recession. 'Of course almost all owners are honest, but there's an old saying which says "freights down, ships down". In other words, when there are so many ships consigned to lay-up berths which may never sail again, it's a temptation to the owner.'

Scuttling is difficult to prove, even when the master and crew are picked up from the ship's lifeboat, dressed in their best suits while their ship appears to have gone down in a calm sea—with her log conveniently missing. Henry Chester and Geoffrey Welch had already told me that every year's account included about ten suspect total losses—around nine of which would usually be paid, because of the cost and difficulty of proving that a ship had been deliberately lost.

Lloyd's most spectacular involvement with a proven case of scuttling came when the 210,000 ton dwt tanker *Salem* sank of Dakar in January 1980. It was the final act of a complex melodrama which began at least three months before, when the fraudsters—one of whom was later identified as an American-Lebanese named Fred Soudan—obtained a purchase contract from the South African Fuel Fund Association (SSF) managed by the South African oil company Sasol to deliver a cargo of crude oil to Durban. Barred by OPEC sanctions from receiving oil through most legitimate channels from the Middle East, Sasol wanted oil at any price, and they agreed to pay $43m for the cargo. On the strength of this contract, the fraudsters obtained an advance from a South African bank, with which they bought the *Salem*.

The fraudsters' next move was to find themselves a cargo. Through a firm of London shipbrokers, they were put in touch with an Italian firm called Pontoil, who had just bought a cargo of 196,000 metric tonnes from the Kuwait government's Ministry of Oil. Pontoil chartered the *Salem* for a voyage to Europe, insuring the cargo on a limited-terms policy, for $56m. At some point during the voyage from Kuwait, Pontoil sold their oil to Shell, on a contract which included the limited-terms insurance of the cargo. Soudan and his team were now set to sell the South Africans the cargo which Shell had already contracted to purchase.

On the day after Boxing Day, 1979, the *Salem*—assumed by her perfectly innocent charterers to be bound for Europe—docked at Durban. One person who happened to notice her was a sharp-eyed marine surveyor who later remembered that he had seen a ship called the *Lema* unloading crude oil. One of the favourite tricks of marine fraudsters is to paint out or add to the letters of a ship's name to disguise her. As a precaution, the *Salem* had become the *Lema*.

During discharge the vessel developed pumping problems—almost certainly the reason why the delivery to Sasol's tanks was of 180,000 metric tonnes instead of the 196,000 metric tonnes the *Salem* had left Kuwait with. Somewhere around the end of the first week of January—presumably the fraudsters decided to cut their losses on the rest of the oil on board for the sake of speed—she was heading for the South Atlantic.

On 17 January she was seen sinking by the BP tanker *British Trident*. Later, when the fraudsters were brought to trial, there were three damning points of evidence against them. One was that, as we have seen, the name of the vessel had been disguised at Durban. The second was the crew's story that explosions had occurred in a fully laden tanker: normally such explosions would only happen on an empty tanker that had not been gas-freed. The third point was that the master of the *British Trident* saw nothing of the gigantic oil slick that would have presumably spread across the ocean had the *Salem* been carrying, as Pontoil believed, a cargo of 196,000 metric tonnes of crude oil.

Lloyd's Intelligence Department's first report of the loss was bad news for underwriters, who faced a possible $24m claim on the *Salem*'s hull, and a further $56m for her cargo. Then, gradually, their solicitors' enquiries began to reveal the real truth—of which further confirmation came when a courageous Tunisian crewman walked into the British Embassy in Paris and asked to talk to someone from Lloyd's of London. Flown to London and installed for several days in what might not be too melodramatically described as a safe house, he unfolded a tale which included such details as that the ship's cook had been instructed to cut, in the early hours of the morning, hundreds of sand-wiches for the crew for a long spell in the lifeboats.

In South Africa, when the true facts became known, Sasol paid Shell $30m for the cargo that had been stolen from them. Meanwhile there was a grey area over the cargo insurers' liability. 'Under the limited conditions of the policy Shell had bought from Pontoil,' explains John Blackwell, LUCRO's Principal Adjuster of cargo claims, 'there was a question as to whether both elements of the cargo loss—the oil unloaded in South Africa and the oil which went down with the *Salem*—had been lost by an insured peril.' Lloyd's and the company underwriters involved felt that their case was strong enough to take to court, but the Queen's Bench Division decided in 1981 that the insurers were liable for both parts of the cargo. Later the Appeal Court ruled that they were not liable for the oil discharged at Durban, and the House of Lords confirmed that the cargo underwriters' eventual liability should be only $3.8m for the cargo that eventually went down.

It was not, however, the complete end of the affair, for the US Justice Department had begun to take an interest in the *Salem*. As a result, Fred Soudan was prosecuted in 1985 and jailed for thirty-five years. Among those who gave evidence at his trial in Houston was LUCRO's John Blackwell. In Greece, a shipping agent and several crew members have also received jail sentences for their part in the fraud. Which is probably the end of the affair. Today, seven years after her loss, Lloyd's underwriters have yet to receive a hull claim on the *Salem*.

Meanwhile there is one other episode which cannot be left out of any account of Lloyd's—not only for its own sake, but because it exemplifies the combination of good taste and gritty professionalism which is the essence of Lloyd's style.

The story of the Indonesian ships—or to be strictly accurate the prologue to it—begins in October 1957. In that month Roy Merrett, a leading war-risk underwriter, was approached by a broker who was trying to place some reinsurance for the newly formed national insurance company of Indonesia, known by its initials as UMUM. The broker was having a certain amount of difficulty in placing the business—could Roy Merrett help?

No Lloyd's underwriter likes to think of good premiums going to waste. At the same time, Roy Merrett, who happened to be a particularly shrewd observer of the world political scene, remembered something he had noted in his diary a year before—that Indonesia was a quarter of the world from which, sooner or later, trouble could be expected. Nevertheless he said he would do what he could for UMUM. Next day, the broker came to his office and introduced Dr Tjoa Sie Hwie, the head of the Indonesian company.

What exactly where the difficulties facing UMUM? Essentially they were implicit in Indonesia's new-found independence. A former colony of the Dutch, it had become a sovereign state under the Hague Agreement of 1949. Though many Dutch business firms had stayed on in the capital, Jakarta, there had lately been rising tension over the territory of Western New Guinea, which had remained under Dutch control by the terms of the Hague Agreement. In 1956, fifteen Afro-Asian states had urged that the question of its independence should go to the United Nations. The previous April, a newly elected Indonesian government, reflecting the increasing nationalistic mood, had set up a Western New Guinea Liberation Committee.

How did all this particularly affect UMUM? Like all national insurance companies in emergent countries, it urgently needed to spread its load of risks by reinsurance. The trouble was that most of the Indonesian links were with Dutch insurers, and by this time relations with Holland were clearly worsening. Moreover, the Dutch underwriters resented the loss of business to UMUM, and refused to help the new company by reinsuring. Dr Tjoa had gone to several other continental insurers, found them unwilling to offend the Dutch, then come on to London. Several broking firms had tried to place the business for him at Lloyd's. But like the continental underwriters, the market did not want to spoil its good relations with the Dutch. Almost as a last throw the broker had approached Roy Merrett.,

From the first moment the two men established a rapport. For the first hour they talked about theosophy, a subject of common interest to them. Merrett decided that Dr Tjoa was a man of integrity that he could work with, and he decided to lead the risk. He put his terms, and Dr Tjoa did not argue. If Merrett thought the terms were fair, that was good enough for him, he told him.

Thus in October 1957 the reinsurance had been placed. Roy Merrett had led the risk and been supported by the market. On October 16 he noted in his diary that Dr Tjoa and his assistant had come to his office to thank him. If he ever had occasion to visit Indonesia, said Dr Tjoa, Roy Merrett would be most welcome.

In Jakarta itself events were now moving fast. In the middle of

November a huge political rally urged the government to take strong action against the Dutch over the Western New Guinea question, and on the last day of the month an attempt was made to assassinate President Soekarno. It was unsuccessful, but triggered off a new wave of nationalism. In the first week of December Dutch-owned banks, hotels and offices were seized by a rioting mob, and the red flag flown from them.

Among the main targets—and it was this which concerned Lloyd's—was the office of the shipping firm KPM. Short for Koninklijke Paketvaart Maatschappij, this was the company operating the main steamer service between the islands that make up the Indonesian archipelago. Most of their fleet was insured in the London market, with the largest share at Lloyd's. On 7 December, *Lloyd's List* carried a brief news item saying that all Dutch ships had been ordered to remain in Indonesian harbours. Within a week half the KPM fleet—around forty ships—had been arrested and were under military control.

At first the Lloyd's market seems scarcely to have reacted. Forty-odd ships lying bottled up in harbour did not, after all, suggest anything as ominous as a total loss. Roy Merrett's own first hint of anxiety came on 6 December, when he noticed that there were rather a lot of brokers around the Room trying to place reinsurance on the KPM fleet. He got the feeling, he noted in his diary, that the Dutch underwriters were getting worried and wanted to unload some of their liability on to the London market.

Why, when the ships were after all in no danger of sinking, should there have been any anxiety at all? The point was that the KPM policies carried one rather unusual clause. Known as the 'four months clause', it had arisen when Dutch owners had become anxious about the possibility of their ships being seized in the Baltic. In the 1950s, the cold war was still on. Dutch brokers have the reputation of being more adroit than most, and it had been a Dutch broker who had noticed that ships trading to countries like Latvia and Finland ran a certain risk of being held by the communists. He had persuaded underwriters to add a clause protecting them from such an arrest for the addition of a tiny extra premium. From then on it had been written into most Dutch policies, including those of the KPM, that if a ship was held for longer than four months, she would count as a total loss.

Now, a week after their seizure, there was no sign of the ships being released. It began to look as if the four months clause might be invoked in a set of circumstances which no one had imagined, and a very long way from the Iron Curtain. The full horror of the situation began to dawn on the Room. In their worst moments, no underwriter had ever imagined the total loss of forty ships of the same fleet. With the complexities of reinsurance nobody quite knew what the possible claim might be, but it was clearly in the range of £11 million; one syndicate alone stood to lose half a million. The marine market began to view things with the nearest Lloyd's ever gets to consternation.

A sub-committee of marine underwriters was formed. On 10 December it was agreed that an approach should be made to the Foreign Office. Basically, Roy Merrett realized, its only chance of getting the ships released hung on one point. If Lloyd's could persuade the Indonesians that by keeping the ships they were hitting at Lloyd's and not the Dutch, then there might be a chance. What was essential was that Lloyd's should be able to put its case to the people who mattered in the Indonesian government.

Someone else who had a line on the ships was a leading marine underwriter named Paul Dixey, later to become Chairman of Lloyd's. At Dunmow in Essex, he had once been to a tea-party with his friend and neighbour Kingsley Martin, then editor of Britain's best-known left-wing weekly, the *New Statesman*. Among the guests had been Dr Subandrio, then Indonesian Ambassador to London. Dixey had talked to him, and later shown him around Lloyd's.

Now, five years later, Dr Subandrio was the Indonesian Foreign Minister. The link seemed tenuous, but potentially useful if, as Merrett and Dixey had already discussed, Lloyd's sent a mission to Jakarta. Nothing else seemed likely to help. *The Times*, in a leader called 'The New Piracy', accused the Indonesian government of playing what it called 'a cat-and-mouse game with the Dutch-owned shipping service that supplies half the islands'. 'Along the KPM wharves,' wrote the paper's Jakarta correspondent on 19 December, 'the ships lie idle in a long silent row . . . while dark-skinned workers sit on their hands beside sheds which are also idle and silent.'

In London, Paul Dixey got a dusty answer from the Foreign Office to the suggestion that a party of underwriters might go out. 'They could hardly have been more damping,' he recalls. 'They said they couldn't possibly be involved in a quarrel between the Indonesians and the Dutch. Beyond that, they were quite certain we hadn't got a chance.'

Meanwhile—and it is at this point that the whole exercise begins to be a particularly immaculate example of Lloyd's combination of self-interest with charm—Roy Merrett had also approached his broker friend who had first introduced him to Dr Tjoa, and reminded him of Dr Tjoa's invitation to stay with him if he ever had occasion to visit Indonesia.

Now, in the last week of December, it began to look as if Roy Merrett might indeed have occasion to visit Indonesia. What would help above all, he decided was a specific invitation. The brokers cabled Dr Tjoa on Merrett's behalf, and on 27 January the reply came back. Would Merrett and some of his friends care to visit Jakarta for the Chinese New Year?

On 11 February the delegation left London. Led by Roy Merrett, it consisted of two other underwriters, Paul Dixey and Harold Hopwood; Hugh Mitchell of Lloyd's Claims Office and A. W. Green of the Commercial Union, which also had a line on the ships. Paul Dixey had taken the trouble to arm himself with letters of introduction from Dorothy Woodman who, besides being Kingsley Martin's wife, was the *New Statesman*'s expert on south-east Asia. 'I remember asking her,' recalls Dixey, 'whether she thought it proper for a leading left-wing journalist to help a group of capitalists. She roared with laughter.'

No sooner had the delegation arrived at Singapore than they struck trouble. The news from Indonesia was that a new coup seemed likely, stemming from the policies of a revolutionary group based on Central Sumatra. The local diplomatic advice was for the delegation to stay put in Singapore and see what happened. Wisely, as things turned out, they ignored it and decided to push on.

By the time they reached Jakarta the threat of the coup had somewhat faded, but the delegation had problems of their own. Roy Merrett, who had planned the whole operation, had been taken ill in Karachi. By now he was in a boiling fever. A Chinese doctor pronounced him suffering from dysentery, and said it would be unthinkable for him to stay as the guest of Dr Tjoa, whose wife was pregnant. Madame Tjoa's reaction was typical of the whole rapport that existed between Lloyd's and the Indonesians—she not only refused to let him leave the house, but nursed him herself till he was over the fever.

Clearly the delegation's presence in Jakarta was officially known, but there was no sign of government reaction. Soon after their arrival Dixey rang up the Foreign Minister's wife and reminded her that they had met in Essex. 'She said how splendid, and that we must come round,' says Dixey. 'After that, we heard nothing.'

For the next few weeks the delegation sat around, answering any questions they were asked about the policy on the ships, and, as one of them put it, 'not muddying the channel'. One day Paul Dixey went to see one of his contacts, a woman who had been secretary to the Cabinet. 'We chatted about everything except the KPM ships,' he recalls. 'At the end of the interview, she asked if I'd been to the port where the ships were—it occurred to her that I might have a special interest in them. She said it with a terrific twinkle.' Looking back, Roy Merrett reflected that one of the main things working to the delegation's advantage had been the general Asian assumption that Britain had displayed considerable intelligence and goodwill over the granting of independence to India. 'I think they contrasted this with the way the Dutch had behaved in Indonesia,' he noted. 'It was one of the things that most helped us.'

Above all there was no hint of a threat, no suggestion that Lloyd's were in a position to damage Indonesia's interests in the future. When the subject of the seized ships did come up, the delegation quietly stated their point that by keeping them, the Indonesians would be harming not the Dutch, but Lloyd's. The last thing the Dutch wanted was the return of forty decaying and damaged ships which were certainly going to be unable to sail the routes for which most of them had been built. Merrett was wryly amused by the element of ironic comedy in their situation. Most British businessmen would have been rushing round trying to contact other British businessmen who knew the ropes out there. Lloyd's was relying on what most people in the City would have called the wrong people.

Each night in the bungalow, Merrett and Dr Tjoa talked over the progress, or lack of it, made each day. Between such talks the delegation spent a lot of time at the UMUM office, helping the company produce a standard policy for hulls. Coming from a group of men whose basic object was to save £11 million, it was a good example of casting your bread upon the waters.

Meanwhile the weeks slipped by, with the April deadline approaching and the four months clause ticking away like a time-bomb. On 10 March Merrett noted in his diary that they didn't feel optimistic. Dixey also began to lose heart: the Indonesians, he felt, were simply stringing them along. 'All they had to do was wait till the four months was up, then Lloyd's would have to pay the loss. After that the ships would become the property of the underwriters, and the best they could hope was that the Indonesians would buy them back cheaply.'

On 12 March, Dr Tjoa told Roy Merrett at their evening conference that the government had come up with a specific request. Urged on by some of their more militant supporters, they wanted confirmation in writing that Lloyd's would be liable for a total loss after the four-month period. It was arranged that Dixey should return to London, show the original policies to the Indonesian Ambassador, then return. After nearly five weeks the delegation seemed almost back to the beginning.

The evening before he was due to go back to London, Dixey rang Madame Subandrio again. 'We still had one ace in our pack, and I decided to play it.' He told her he was going back to London and was sorry to do so without seeing her husband.

'But he *does* want to see you.' She would ring her husband at his office now, Madame Subandrio said, then ring Dixey back at UMUM.

Dixey hung around the UMUM office for more than an hour. It was just on midday, and the whole of Jakarta was about to close down. Meanwhile he wanted to get some presents to take home, and flowers for people who had been helpful in Jakarta. In the absence of a phone call from the Foreign Minister's wife, he decided to go and get them before the shops shut. He left the office, went down a couple of staircases, then remembered he hadn't got the address of someone he wanted to send flowers to. He went back upstairs to the empty office, found the address, and was just about to leave again when the phone rang. It was Madame Subandrio. Would Dixey call round that evening before he left and bring his friends?

Back at Dr Tjoa's house, the delegation held a council of war—even now, they were convinced there was little chance of anything happening. In the evening Merrett, Dixey and Harold Hopwood set off in drenching rain. In the car on the way Roy Merrett gave the others a piece of advice which summed up the delegation's approach. 'Remember,' he said, 'we'll play it our way. We're not going to mention those ships.'

When they arrived at the Foreign Minister's villa, Dr Subandrio gave them a glass of orange juice, enquired after mutual friends and then asked why Dixey was going back to London. Dixey said he was going to produce some insurance policies for the Ambassador there, and Dr Subandrio looked surprised.

'Then he said the words I'll never forget,' says Dixey. 'He said, "But you know we're going to give you back those ships." I don't know how low you can get and then go whizzing up to the heights. But that's what we did.'

In the event it took another month before the matter of the forty ships was settled. Dixey returned to London and showed the Ambassador the policies. On 20 March Roy Merrett, who stayed on with the others in Jakarta, recorded in his diary: 'Dr Tjoa came in with great news.' It was that the government had officially decreed the release of the ships. On 22 March, *Lloyd's List* reported, in characteristically deadpan style, that Indonesia had 'formally handed back thirty-four impounded ships of N.V. Koninklijke Paketvaart Maatschappij'.

A week later the delegation went down to the Tandjong Docks and drank a farewell glass of orange juice with one of the Dutch captains. Merrett said to the Captain how delighted he must be to be going, and for the first time in all the Lloyd's team's jubilation there was a note of sadness. The captain said he'd been in Indonesia a very long time and he minded going. One of the Indonesians who was there said he was sorry to see him go as well. In the midst of all the trouble, Merrett sensed, there had been some very real relationships.

But by now the saga of the Indonesian ships was almost over. On 31 March Merrett cruised round the harbour in a launch watching the last of the vessels being got ready for sailing. Three days later he sent a telex to Lloyd's confirming that they had all left, except one which had mechanical trouble at Surabaya, and three others which were still in outlying ports.

The whole episode had some agreeable by-products. When the delegation got back to Lloyd's, they were given a presentation by the Room. The following year Lloyd's underwriters were able to make a return gesture to the Indonesian government over a difficult insurance on tobacco products, and relations continue to flourish. Roy Merrett became the godfather of Madame Tjoa's baby. For years afterwards he visited the family and the picture of his godson occupied a prominent position on his mantlepiece, next to the clock given him by his grateful colleagues in the Room.

In the end the Indonesian affair could be called the definitive exercise in Lloyd's style. It is also probably the only major commercial deal in history which depended on a talk about theosophy, a tea party in an Essex village and a bunch of flowers.

There is an agreeable pendant to the tale of the KPM ships. Coincidentally, it also relates to Indonesia. But the reason for telling it here is that it concerns another Merrett, and his writing of satellite insurance.

In the early days of space exploration, Lloyd's aviation underwriters had been the pioneers of such risks. Then, when the loss of an $85m satellite in 1979 was accompanied by falling rates, many syndicates pulled out of the market. The market's confidence was shaken by more losses in 1984 and 1985—most notably in February 1984, when two Model 376 satellites, one belonging to Western Union and the other to the Indonesian government, failed to go into orbit and were left floating purposelessly in space.

One Lloyd's man who had never lost his confidence in space projects was a marine underwriter named Stephen Merrett; the son of the Roy Merrett who figured in the saga of the Indonesian ships. He was one of those who had reinsured the Western Union satellite. What occurred to Merrett was a piece of Lloyd's panache worthy of its long tradition. Since underwriters were being asked to pay the claim on the now uselessly spinning spacecraft, Merrett reasoned, they were entitled to claim it as a piece of salvage. If it should prove possible to recover either or both the craft, they could be sold as a means of reducing the underwriters' losses.

In the autumn of 1984 Merrett signed a series of agreements on behalf of a group of underwriters which effectively gave them the rights of disposal of the satellites. These followed a further agreement with the Hughes Aircraft Co and NASA for an unprecedented voyage of the Shuttle *Discovery*. The mission, in which five astronauts were to take part, would aim to recover both satellites and bring them back to earth for refurbishment.

Stephen Merrett was among those who watched *Discovery* touch down at the Kennedy Space Centre in Florida on 16 November 1984 after what turned out to be a memorable journey. Later, he heard from astronaut Joseph Allen how he had had to make a complete circuit of the Earth while holding one of the two recaptured satellites triumphantly—but rather painfully since he had cramp in his arms during the one-and-a-half hour circuit—above him. The exploit of the five astronauts—they included Dr Anna Fisher who had become the first mother to go into space—had an unusual sequel at the White House two months later. On 7 December 1984 a presentation of the Lloyd's Silver Medal was made to the astronauts by President Reagan—the first time the Medal had ever been presented by someone other than a Lloyd's man.

The New Lloyd's: the Lime Street entrance

Astronaut manoeuvres satellite back to *Discovery*—the feat which earned Lloyd's Silver Medal

The **Adam Room** where the Council of Lloyd's meets. The tables are laid for lunch in honour of HM the Queen when she opened the New Lloyd's in November 1986

10

The New Lloyd's

In 1769, when Angerstein and his fellow-underwriters moved with Thomas Fielding to the Pope's Head Alley coffee-house, they called themselves the New Lloyd's. For some while the name remained in use, to distinguish the new and re-organized coffee-house from the den of gambling underwriters who had almost ruined Lloyd's name. Four years later, when Angerstein and his friends took over the lease of the original two rooms in the Royal Exchange, they signed it 'for themselves and the rest of the Committee of the New Lloyd's'.

Recently the name has again come into use. One reason may be that 'the new building' seems somehow too pedestrian a phrase to convey the uniqueness and dominance of the Rogers design.

But there is also another reason, and a more profound one: a desire to move away from the scandals of 1982, almost as if the market needed to recapture the relief with which Angerstein and his friends put the memory of the gambling days behind them.

It was therefore a good deal more than a convenient phrase when, on 17 November 1986, Lloyd's Chairman Peter Miller invited the Queen 'to open, not just another Lloyd's building, but the New Lloyd's'.

Perhaps the first thing to be said about Rogers' spectacular design is that the New Lloyd's is far less like an office than a theatre—in which the underwriters who occupy the ground floor and the first three galleries are the actors. The building is therefore very much a whole design, constructed round a central atrium whose glass-walled galleries lead up to the great barrel vault which is its dominating feature. The walls themselves are partly made of see-through glass, while other sections are designed to react to sunlight. Externally, six satellite towers house stairs, toilets and equipment, while wondering passers-by in Leadenhall Street can watch the brokers going up and down in glass-sided lifts which are the first in London to be outside a building.

But factual description does little justice to the fantasy of silvery steel and glass which has added a dimension of delight to humdrum Leadenhall Street. Viewed simply as a work of art, it grows on you by glimpses. Seen from London Bridge, for example, the great semi-circle of glass round the atrium has created a new focus of interest on the City skyline. Look down on the Room from the eleventh floor, and your wrong-end-of-the-telescope view of the Cooper Rostrum will give you a new and unnerving experience of spatial vision. Or stand on the ground floor by the Rostrum and look up—the sense of over-whelming space above you will be tangible and awesome.

Why did Richard Rogers design the New Lloyd's as he did? It is worth recalling how, on the first page of this book, we saw that the heart and centre of Lloyd's is a room called simply *the* Room. Design-ing a home for Lloyd's is entirely different from designing an office building—what the market basically requires is space for underwriting. Thus Rogers' conception of a building turned inside-out goes to the heart of what is needed. The lifts are not put outside in order to give brokers a dizzying view of City steeples—but to save precious square feet. The result is a building of which sixty-five per cent of the space is actually used, as against forty per cent in the 1958 Room. Flexibility is another factor. Should more underwriting space be needed in years to come, any or all of the galleries above the present three can be brought into the market.

For Lloyd's, the decision to go ahead with Rogers' design called for both nerve and imagination. The realization that the market needed more space came in the mid-1970s, when what was then known as the Old Room—the Underwriting Room to which Lloyd's had moved from the Royal Exchange in 1928—was still in use as offices, while the main Room—the 1958 building, was on the other side of Lime Street. Why not, thought the Lloyd's Committee, refurbish the Old Room and bring it back into service as an extension of the main Room?

At first the idea seemed attractive. A rough costing of £15m was thought of. But then some forward-looking members of the Com-mittee began to have doubts about using the Old Room merely as an annexe. One of them was Ian Findlay, who later became Chairman. Talking one day to a senior member of the Corporation staff, Findlay suddenly threw up his hands. 'Here we are planning to spend fifteen million on refurbishing the Old Room. And in another twenty years we're going to run out of space again. If we do this we're barmy.'

Future generations of underwriters seem likely to owe a considerable debt of gratitude to Findlay's sudden insight. As a result of it, various working parties were set up, and Courtenay Blackmore, then Lloyd's Head of Administration and a most unbureaucratic administrator, was put in charge of planning. In 1977 a competition was held, in which six of the world's leading architectural partnerships were asked to undertake a four-month study of Lloyd's needs and then to produce a design to meet them. The only essentials, the architects were told, was that the design must be for a single marketplace, and that the site must be in what has been, for the last sixty years, the heart of the insurance world—the narrow thoroughfare of Lime Street.

The eventual choice of Richard Rogers' design was made in close collaboration with the RIBA, while the Royal Fine Arts Commission congratulated Lloyd's on a 'most enlightened piece of architectural patronage'. Underwriters and brokers studied models of the new design with a mixture of puzzlement, wonder and some derision too. At first, only the more perceptive of older underwriters accepted the boldness of the concept. There were jokes about Lloyd's having started in a coffee-house and, after 300 years, having got the percolator. For most of the younger generation, though, curiosity soon turned to admiration as they began to perceive that the new building was going to enhance Lloyd's reputation for style and individualism. When building actually began in 1981, it was the first time since Wren that a major architect had been given the chance of making such an impact on the City.

'A landmark on the London skyline and in the history of Lloyd's' was how the Queen described it at the opening five years later. Afterwards she and the Duke of Edinburgh saw not only the new marvels but many of the famous symbols of the old Lloyd's, for one of the features of the design is that it has incorporated some of the resplendent showpieces which are part of the tradition. The Nelson silver, for example was somewhat tucked away in a small museum in the 1958 Room. In the New Lloyd's, it has been brought out into the main concourse where it is much more generally on show. The panelled library, built for the 1928 Room, has been preserved intact and re-erected within a few yards of its old site. Both the Bowood House Committee room and Sir Edwin Cooper's rostrum have, as we saw earlier, been preserved, while another touch of local history has been added by the building of what is in effect a new City street on the east side of the New Lloyd's. Leading from Leadenhall Street to Leadenhall Market, it has been named the Green Yard, commemorating the garden of the same name that, the records tell us, adjoined the mediaeval manor of Sir Hugh Nevill, the founder of the market.

As to the Captains' Room, the new restaurant and buffet on the concourse floor are still known by the old name—though some of its former visitors might find the consumption of claret modest by their standards. 'Nowadays,' one broker told me, 'ninety per cent of the underwriters won't drink over lunch. They're back at their boxes after an hour and a half, and most of the lunchtime talk is business.' That, too, perhaps, is part of the New Lloyd's.

What the new Room has above all achieved is the collaboration of the high-tech world with Lloyd's tradition. The computers sit easily with the Lutine Bell, and after three hundred years the design is still built around the coffee-house tradition. With his overheads at a fraction of those of a conventional company in terms of occupying expensive space, the underwriter's box is not merely a ritual symbol. It is Lloyd's secret weapon in the world's competitive markets.

'I think it's rather nice,' said one young and not particularly respectful underwriter, 'to think of the Chairman sitting up there, looking down on the market. It makes him part of the place, in a way that he wasn't in the old Room.'

It is indeed possible for Peter Miller, from his twelfth floor eyrie, to look down in Olympian style on the tiny pepperpot of the Rostrum and the escalators that from that height look like caterpillars. But in practice the Chairman of Lloyd's has not too much time for idle gazing. 'Besides,' says Peter Miller, 'it's not good for the Chairman to be treated as too god-like. It's important to avoid the sin of *hubris*.'

The classical sin of overweening pride is not one which most people would connect with Peter Miller, whose relaxed style and mental agility have made him the most popular as well as the most effective of Lloyd's recent Chairmen. He has needed to be both, for his four years in office have coincided with the post-Cameron Webb period in which he has held the market together when its walls must often have seemed to be crumbling around him.

Bespectacled and disarmingly youthful-looking for fifty-six, he looks almost too much of an intellectual to be the holder of a major City office. He points out the treasures of the Chairman's room in un-Olympian style, more like a custodian than an owner. There are the two splendid eighteenth century naval swords, the small Lawrence drawing of Angerstein, and a superb sea-fight scene from the War of

Jenkins' Ear. One of his predecessors, he said, had taken the first news of that naval victory to Downing Street, though he didn't see himself fulfilling quite the same role. At the far end of the room hang two large and lovingly-framed Georgian sea-charts; they had been, he said, a housewarming present from the Governor of the Bank of England. 'He decided to create an instant tradition by which the Bank gives us a present each time Lloyd's moves.'

Peter Miller came into the Lloyd's market after reading history at Oxford, where he distinguished himself as a runner and as a budding lawyer. But his family had long connections with marine insurance. His great-grandfather, Thomas Miller, had founded the firm which still manages the largest of the shipowners' mutual associations—known as Protecting and Indemnity or P and I Clubs—which had been set up in the nineteenth century to provide the owners with liability cover they could not get elsewhere in the market. Alongside the P and I Clubs, there had sprung up the Lloyd's broking firm of Thomas R. Miller (Insurance), who, though general brokers, have always specialized in placing reinsurance for the mutuals, and it is in this firm that Peter Miller has spent his Lloyd's life.

As a historian he draws some interesting insights from his family connections. Recently, he said, he had come across a cashbook which his great-grandfather had kept in the 1890s. 'He was a lawyer and manager of a P and I Club, and the cashbook included everything from the club finances to the gardener's wages. You could do business like that in those days. An underwriter would simply send his names a cheque with a letter saying, "Dear Smith, here's a cheque." That was very appropriate for a syndicate where all the members were in the City and all knew each other. But it wouldn't be appropriate for Lloyd's today, or indeed any time over the last twenty-five years.'

All this, he said, was very relevant to the question he was always being asked: had Lloyd's, especially from the point of view of the names, now truly put its house in order? 'You can't be certain, if you trade at Lloyd's, that you won't lose money. But a name—who today is often physically far removed from Lime Street—is trading in a well-regulated market. In contrast to my great-grandfather's homely cashbook, there's a whole array of information to make him better-informed about the market. But a prospective name should use his native shrewdness to pick a good underwriting agent. Nobody who comes to Lloyd's should believe there's any substitute for their own judgment when it comes to that.'

We turned to the question of new forms of business for the market which were, he said, a marvellously varied pattern. 'In ten years Lloyd's has built up a major stake in the United Kingdom motor market because we went in for direct dealing. Binding authorities in Canada have taken us into a whole range of new household insurance markets. The challenge is to perceive market niches where we can go in and do things at a profit.'

Though China could hardly be described as a niche, one of the historic events of Peter Miller's Chairmanship was (see p. 67) his 1985 tour of ten major Chinese cities. 'I think it was Paul Dixey who said that one of the roles of a Chairman of Lloyd's is to open doors which others can go through. The links we set up with the PICC will be of great importance when the Chinese need, as I believe they will, to protect their domestic book against catastrophe by the kind of high-level reinsurance cover at which Lloyd's is particularly expert.'

The Lloyd's visit to China was especially helped by the fact that Miller's Chinese wife Leni, who was born in Kuala Lumpur, speaks fluent Cantonese—more fluent, in fact, than he had realized till they got to China. 'It was her intuitive understanding of Chinese attitudes,' he said, 'which gave our whole party the clue when to stop being merely charming and appreciative visitors, and to make it clear that we were there on serious business. She took me on one side, saying that the moment had come to make it clear what we hoped to achieve in terms of business.' It so happened that the party's next engagement was a meeting with the Governor of Fukien province, who began his greeting by saying 'I am a small and hungry man'. Miller, who has no hang-ups about his less-than-average height, promptly came back: 'I am smaller and even hungrier.' From that moment, he says, the tour took off in terms of serious talk of business.

I asked about the future of syndicates at Lloyd's since they can no longer be owned by brokers. Peter Miller's view is that the underwriting agency system had been seriously weakened by the sale of syndicates to brokers: his own firm, following the pattern of the John Lewis department stores is owned as a partnership which embodies an employee's trust. We spoke of Frank Barber's views on partnership, mentioned earlier in this book, and Miller nodded warmly. 'Those who are generating profits should enjoy the fruits of their labours.'

Peter Miller's sense of style is coupled with one other attribute unusual in the business world—he is something of a showman. It was his own idea that 'some great music' should be included in the programme for the royal opening of the New Lloyd's, and few who heard Sir Charles Groves conducting Haydn's Nelson Mass in the new Room could fail to be grateful for the inspiration. 'If I hadn't been Chairman of Lloyd's,' says Miller with evident relish, 'how would I have met the President of the United States or proposed the toast to HM the Queen with her sitting there beside me?'

His speeches, which he writes himself, all bear his own stamp—often an imaginative one, as in his speech at the opening of the New Lloyd's. When President Reagan decided he would like to present Lloyd's silver medals to the *Discovery* astronauts, who included, as we saw earlier, Dr Anna Lee Fisher, Miller wondered if it might be the first time the award for meritorious services had been given to a woman. His researches disproved this but were nevertheless unusually apt. A fortnight later in Washington, he was able to tell the President and the astronauts how yet another historic link between Lloyd's and the United States was being repeated. 'This is a day of firsts,' he told them. 'It is the first time that the medal has been awarded for a salvage in space. It is the first time that anyone other than the Chairman or a representative of Lloyd's has made such a presentation. It is the first time that five medals have been awarded at one time. Mr President, it is not, however, the first time that the medal has been awarded to a lady. Let me briefly tell you the story. In July 1896, there sailed from Hong Kong an iron sailing ship bound for New York, Westabout. Blown hundreds of miles off course, the captain decided to turn on his heel and make passage via Cape Horn rather than the Cape of Good Hope. Disease decimated his crew. The mate and bosun were washed overboard by the mountainous seas of the Horn. The captain and his wife alone survived and alone brought the ship to her destination in March 1897, and the captain's wife was awarded Lloyd's silver medal for her incredible hardihood. But, sir, the *T. F. Oakes* was an American ship and the master's wife, Mrs Reed, an American lady. So Dr Fisher is treading in patriotic footsteps.'

I said goodbye to the Chairman and strolled across to the Committee Room whose glittering chandeliers and Adam fireplace seemed to fit unexpectedly but happily into Richard Rogers' world of high-tech—as felicitously, I thought, as Peter Miller's speech in the Roosevelt Room of the White House had linked space travel with the maritime world that Lloyd's is never far from. I remembered, too, the words of Thomas Taylor, eighteenth century master of the coffee-house: 'The management of this house has ever been the pride of my heart'.

Two hundred years later, I thought, the management was still in safe hands.

I went into the Room for a last look round—the great Room whose occupants over the years have coloured the world of commerce with originality and a touch of romance, and added the dimension of style to the business of making money. It was after half past four. Except for a small queue at a leading underwriter's box, the stream of brokers was thinning.

On the casualty boards the yellow, pink and blue notices announced the day's consignment of destruction—floods, fires, earthquakes, riots. An underwriter and a broker were looking at them. After a moment somebody came up and showed a note to the underwriter, who nodded, then turned to the broker.

'We had an arrival,' he said, and the broker laughed. They might have been talking about anything from the safe landing of a cargo to the opening of a trade fair, but the old maritime phrase seemed to span Lloyd's history.

Whatever it was that had arrived, it was time for my departure. I said goodbye to the waiter on the door, and went out into the winter sunlight.

The Lutine Bell
hangs from the
Rostrum designed by
Sir Edwin Cooper for
the 1928 Room

Peter Miller shows
HM the Queen
round the Visitors'
Gallery and
Exhibition

The Atrium

Opening Day of the New Room on 17 November 1986: HM the Queen with architect Richard Rogers

A Layman's Guide to Insurance Terms

Assured   Anyone whose life or property is protected by insurance. Although the words insurance and assurance are interchangeable the latter is used more often in connection with life business.

Audit   Lloyd's Audit was introduced in 1908 with the object of ensuring the individual solvency of the underwriting accounts of all Members of Lloyd's.

Broker   An insurance broker places insurance on behalf of a client. As the agent of the insured his job is to obtain the best terms he can. His only obligations to underwriters, by whom he is paid on a commission basis, are those of good faith and responsibility for premiums.

Captive   Used in the same sense as a captive audience. Some large organizations paying considerable sums in premiums have found it worthwhile to set up a company specifically to handle their insurance. Examples are to be found within ICI and among a number of the big oil companies.

Consequential Loss   A fire which destroys a factory could, in addition to the cost of rebuilding, mean a loss of profits to the owner. A normal fire policy might cover plant and machinery, but consequential insurance would also compensate the owner for any loss of revenue.

Correspondent   A local broker, usually in the United States, who can place business in the market through a Lloyd's broker.

Deductible   The specified proportion of any claim which is to be borne by the assured: for example, most motor insurance policies specify that the insured will pay the first £10 of any claim.

Excess of Loss   A form of reinsurance (*q.v.*) by which an underwriter can protect himself against loss above a given amount. This type of business is often done in layers involving more than one reinsurer. For example, an underwriter having written a risk for £100,000 may wish to limit his liability to, say, £20,000. He can do this by getting another underwriter to cover him for £20,000 for any claim in excess of £20,000. Then he might get a third underwriter to cover the remaining £20,000. Thus a claim for £50,000 would cost the first underwriter £20,000, the second £20,000 and the third £10,000. Excess of loss reinsurance was devised by C. E. Heath following heavy claims arising from the San Francisco earthquake.

Hull   For insurance purposes this is the ship itself excluding the engines. Underwriters also speak of the 'hull' of an aircraft.

Infidelity   Not, as one underwriter explained, what they mean by it in Knightsbridge, but a breach of trust on the part of an employee.

Line   The amount of an underwriter's liability. They write and initial the proportion of the risk they are willing to accept on one line of a slip.

Lloyd's Agent   Agents of the Corporation of Lloyd's. Their primary duty is to keep Lloyd's informed of shipping movements, casualties and other matters of interest to insurers and the commercial community generally. They also survey damaged cargo and some agents have authority to settle cargo claims.

Lloyd's Underwriting Agency   A Lloyd's underwriter will accept risks on behalf of many names, but his staff, accounts and investment of premium income will all need management. This is provided by underwriting agency companies. The underwriting agency does not accept risks but fulfils a purely administrative function.

Loading   An increase in premium to cover an increase in risk. A larger premium, for instance, may be required for young or inexperienced motorists.

Name   A term usually applied to an underwriting member of Lloyd's who need not necessarily be actively engaged in the market, but participates as a 'name' on a syndicate.

Policy Legal evidence of the agreement to insure which may be produced by the insured in court to press a claim against the insurer.

Premium   The sum of money paid by the assured to the insurer in return for compensation in the event of loss from an insured peril.

Premium Income   Income derived by underwriters from their premiums. The current annual premium income of Lloyd's is now well in excess of £6 billion.

Producer   Another word for correspondent (*q.v.*).

Reinsurance   When an underwriter has written a line on a slip he becomes liable for any loss which may occur on that insurance. He may seek to lay off some of his liability by insuring it in turn with other underwriters who then become his reinsurers.

Slip   A slip of paper used by brokers for placing an insurance. It contains brief details of the risk on which underwriters write their lines. The slip was formerly a somewhat undisciplined document but a standardized version has now gained acceptance.

Syndicate   For practical reasons members of Lloyd's group themselves into syndicates. Some syndicates consist of hundreds of members, some of only a handful. Some are specialists in one class of risk; most write a broad spread of business.

Underwriter   One who accepts liability for insurance. The name is derived from the time-honoured practice by which underwriters write their names one under another on the slip. Usually implies a member of Lloyd's, but can be a paid employee of either a Lloyd's syndicate or an insurance company who works as an underwriter.

War Risks   Technically these include capture, seizure, arrest, restraint or detainment of princes or peoples, men of war, engines of war, mines, torpedoes or any hostile act. War risks on land is one of the very few insurances which may not be underwritten at Lloyd's or by any commercial body.

Wet Risks   A phrase spanning the somewhat grey area between marine and non-marine. A non-marine risk having the smell of the sea about it such as dams, piers, wharves and bridges.

(The above glossary is reprinted by courtesy of Robert H. Brown.)

Index